AMAZING
PLACES
COST
NOTHING

HERBERT YPMA

AMAZING PLACES COST NOTHING

THE NEW GOLDEN AGE OF AUTHENTIC TRAVEL

Thames & Hudson

CONTENTS

INTRODUCTION

Originally I was going to describe this book as 'the result of twenty years' work' but to label twenty years of travel and adventure as 'work' seemed odd. 'Twenty years of travel and adventure' isn't accurate either. The truth is – much as I would like to credit the amazing places in this book to a keen eye and tireless lust for travel – most of them were discovered by accident.

You couldn't plan a collection like this. It's not the result of a Great Book Idea or a focused Google search. The stories don't follow a formula, and I swear that none of the details have been fabricated. They simply relate how I happened to stumble upon each of these astonishing places: by getting 'ambushed' at an airport, lost in a crocodile-infested mangrove swamp at night, stuck out at sea in a rowboat, carried down a raging river on a broken-down ferry, etc. There is no substitute for the wonderful randomness of all these happy accidents, spread over twenty years and ranging across the globe.

As a result, this book probably gets closer to a true travel tome than any I have ever attempted before. Real travel is emotive and deeply satisfying and, out of all the things we experience in our lives, certainly one of the most memorable and enduring pursuits. But today, with all the convenience of modern travel and the reassuring familiarity of an increasingly globalized world, authentic adventure and discovery are getting ever more difficult to find. Three or four hundred years ago you only had to throw a dart at a world map and you could guarantee that you would arrive in a place that was utterly strange and exciting. Now homogeneous global brands dominate what we eat, what we drive, what we wear, and what we watch and listen to, and large parts of the world are beginning to look very much the same. This makes the discovery of a place that is truly unique that much more valuable.

This book isn't intended as a guide to cheap travel – there are plenty such books out there and they date quickly – but as a poignant reminder that the world's most amazing places intrinsically cost nothing, and the most exciting and authentic places to stay while you visit them don't cost much more. The hotels and resorts collected here are the best of a rare breed: undiscovered treasures that only reluctantly reveal themselves to outsiders, yet at the same time tantalizingly accessible as they offer such exceptional value for money. These are the places we all dream about: with real personality, free of formulaic branding and situated in mesmerizing locations that make you realize just how amazing this planet can still be.

I don't think you ever forget these sorts of places; I certainly haven't. Twenty years on I didn't need a single note or scrap of reference material to be able to remember each and every detail about them. From the rainforests of Brazil to the wineries of South Africa to a forgotten island in the Gulf of Siam, these hidden gems are capable of surprising even the well-seasoned traveller with their beauty, unspoiled authenticity and refreshing affordability. One could argue that by publishing this collection of amazing places, I am in effect spoiling them. But I am a big believer in the philosophy that it is always better to share knowledge than keep it locked away.

TRANCOSO
BRAZIL
ETNIA POUSADA

*Colour, charm and Latin cool combine
in the verdant centre of Brazil's
capital of hippy chic*

T rancoso is the Bali of Brazil. People are laid-back (hardly anyone wears shoes or a shirt), the ambience is fun and unpretentious, the surroundings are lush and unspoiled and the culture is as authentic as it gets.

Situated on a pristine stretch of Brazil's Bahia coastline, Trancoso is dotted with worn and faded wooden fishing shacks painted in an array of vibrant colours, as you might expect to find in a tropical South American country. There are no throbbing night-clubs or decadent beach restaurants where bored bankers spray each other with expensive champagne. Nor is there any traffic – everyone walks everywhere. People ride horses on the beach, swim in the tur-quoise waters and hang out in the *quadrado*, a grass-covered sandy square (it is actually a long rectangle, but who wants to be pedantic in Paradise?) with a picturesque whitewashed church at one end. If the aim is to chill, then it's hard to imagine a better place.

The appeal of Trancoso is in its DNA. In the 1960s and 1970s, this beautiful little fishing village was a favourite with hippies. Slowly, as word got out, Trancoso became a fashionable destination. Wealthy visitors from São Paulo and glam socialites from Rio started to hang out with the sandal-wearing, beaded, dreadlocked locals. The bil-lionaires became hippies, and the hippies became rich. The crowd changed but the vibe didn't.

Success has adapted to Trancoso, rather than the other way around. There are no high-rise mega-hotels, shopping malls, water

parks, aquariums or casinos, and I doubt there ever will be. There was talk of build-ing an airport outside the centre but the residents voted against it, and now that Trancoso is a UNESCO World Heritage Site, it seems unlikely that the proposal will be reconsidered in the future. With its quaint fishing shacks, lush jungle back-drops and idyllic beaches, this town has retained its original charm and contin-ues to attract sophisticated visitors with simple tastes.

Viewed from a plane, the beaches are mesmerizing: long stretches of pale sand framed by a dense green border of jungle and turquoise water that slowly morphs into the dark azure of the Atlantic. And there is hardly a building in sight. I arrived, after a 45-minute drive from Seguro, hoping to stay on the beach and, if I am entirely honest, was some-what disappointed to discover that most of the accommodation is arranged near or around the *quadrado*. However, it doesn't take long to understand that this is part of the magic of the place: it keeps the beach clean and unspoiled and focuses all social activities, includ-ing eating and drinking, around the *quadrado*.

Tucked away in the lush green of the jungle, just a short stroll from the *quadrado*, lies a compound called Etnia Pousada, which, with its bright colours, ethnic touches and relaxed approach, seems like a miniature Trancoso within Trancoso itself. Guests stay in indi-vidual bungalows, each of which has its own special character. Some have yellow trim, others blue or red, echoing the bright but faded patinas of the fishing shacks. The overall effect is a seemingly

effortless style of decor that is at once familiar, exotic and comfortable.

Staying at Etnia Pousada is like visiting a rich uncle with impeccable taste. The proprietors, Italian Conrado Tini and Brazilian-born Italian Andre Zanonato, run the place as if it were their home. Both have professional backgrounds in fashion and design: Tini used to work for Jean Paul Gaultier while Zanonato made his living from ceramics. One day the two decided that they had had enough of the rat race. They bought a piece of land and then spent two years creating a series of bungalows set in a tropical garden where there had once been only jungle.

Guests eat, meet and swim in the centrally located pool pavilion. Although the compound does not have a full service restaurant, the hosts take great pride in the presentation of breakfast and afternoon tea. As a guest you feel not only warmly welcomed but also quite spoiled. After a few days at Etnia Pousada, I was struck by what a perfect base it is for enjoying everything Trancoso has to offer. You have peace, serenity and seclusion when you want it, and lively barefoot dining available nearby in any number of the converted shacks around the *quadrado* when you don't.

The beach is walking distance but not that close – more like a 10-minute walk – which is normal for Trancoso, where everyone walks to the beach. You will find yourself bumping into the same people over and over again along the paths that lead through the jungle. The daily trek (mini-trek, really) to the beach becomes a social experience that encapsulates Trancoso's friendly, laid-back vibe and makes it easy to reconnect with the natural beauty of Brazil, which surely is the point of visiting it in the first place.

When I first arrived at Etnia Pousada, I was probably like most Trancoso first-timers. I loved what I saw but didn't feel entirely comfortable walking around without a shirt, particularly when it came to having lunch or dinner. It went against my whole upbringing. I remembered the time when my teenage sister brought home a new tattooed boyfriend who had not bothered to wear a shirt for the occasion, and my father was so incensed that he complained about it for a month, until my sister finally got fed up and said, 'You're just upset because he has a great body and you don't.' They should carve these words into a sign as you enter Trancoso.

Let's face it: most of the things we do in our everyday lives make no sense at all. Getting rid of shoes and shirt is liberating, and in a strange way it is the ultimate luxury. In any event, it is certainly the key to enjoying Trancoso. Lose the shirt and you lose your inhibitions. Before long you will find yourself dancing barefoot in the *quadrado* after a very spirited (literally) dinner, demonstrating that the samba really does *not* come naturally to everyone. Trancoso is convincing proof of how little we really need in order to be able to unwind completely. And who among us isn't drawn by the idea of being shirtless and carefree in the birthplace of Brazilian hippy chic?

From a palette of simple ingredients
including polished concrete, draped
muslin and vibrant paint, Etnia Pousada
has crafted its own distinctive style. Each
guest has a private bungalow and each
bungalow is different, but all share the
same sense of effortless chic.

Set in a patch of dense jungle a few minutes' walk from the beach,
Etnia Pousada consists of a compound of small villas. The most centrally
placed villa, which sits adjacent to the pool, is where people meet and eat.
In the morning it's the setting for breakfast; during the day there's enough of
a clearing to sunbathe by the pool and in the evening it's the perfect place
for an aperitif before heading out to the nearby *quadrado* with its brightly
coloured fishermen's cottages that have been converted into restaurants.

LUANG PRABANG
LAOS
THE APSARA

Industrial legacy meets ethnic edge in a
converted warehouse on the banks
of the Mekong River

Luang Prabang is a weird and wonderful place. The Coen brothers should do a film here. Without a doubt, it makes for one of the most eccentric weekend breaks in Asia.

The adventure starts with an hour-long flight from Bangkok. On arrival, you are ushered into an old-fashioned Communist-style reception area with lots of red tape, uniforms and a colonial-era level of bureaucracy. You hand in your passport, which disappears behind a very long, tall partition, and a voice from behind the screen yells out your name. Then, in a scene reminiscent of Thing from *The Addams Family*, a hand returns your passport over the wall. In my case, it came back in two pieces.

With the visa pages in one hand and the all-important chip-encoded data page in the other, I had plenty of reason to panic. I was scheduled to visit another five countries in Asia over the next five weeks and now my passport was in pieces. 'Who did this?' I screamed. Not the cleverest thing to do in a sombre military airport. No one came forward (hardly a surprise) so I decided to take matters into my own hands. I grabbed a chair, dragged it up to the partition, climbed on it, and started waving my vandalized passport at the slightly shocked civil servants sitting on the other side. They were not amused by the sight of a crazed foreigner shouting at them and I was promptly arrested.

That's how I ended up in a detention room at Luang Prabang's airport with a colonel in a fancy uniform adorned with copious red stars and gold buttons yelling at me. He was like a character straight out of *The Bridge on the River Kwai* (the bad guy, not the hero). 'You bad man,' he bellowed. 'You not respect uniform, you not respect our country.' He was right about the uniform.

'Look what you did to my passport,' I barked indignantly, waving the pages in his face. Not a good idea – neither the waving nor the barking.

'Oh,' he replied, softly, inspecting it closely as if I had never been through the arrival procedure, 'This passport not normal. Why document page not attached? This not legal.'

Oops – game over! I had just given him the perfect excuse to detain me in jail and then deport me. Time to go into 'crawl' mode.

'I'm sorry, I don't know what got into me,' I said. 'I've really been travelling too much and I'm very tired. That's why my passport has a lot of wear and tear. Don't worry about it – I'll get a new one at the embassy in Bangkok. Nice uniform, by the way.'

The colonel basked in my climb-down, and then let me go.

Meanwhile, my host Ivan had been patiently waiting for me in the arrival hall. Ivan Scholte, who doesn't look or sound like an Ivan – he speaks like Prince Charles and resembles Roger Moore – used to be a wine importer in Hong Kong. That was before he chucked it all in, bought a place in Luang Prabang overlooking the Mekong River and converted it into a charming hotel.

According to Ivan, I had been lucky. 'They don't need much incentive to lock you away', he told me in an 'I've seen it all before' tone of voice. But as we drove further away from the airport, pondering my lucky escape from the colonel and the formidable bureaucracy of the Lao People's Revolutionary Party, I began to understand what had been the attraction for Ivan in moving to this place.

Luang Prabang is a jewel – one of the best-preserved outposts of the former French Indochine – with a remarkable collection of beautiful colonial houses and a population of 5,000 Buddhist monks. Built on a peninsula that juts out into the snaking curves of the Mekong River, the town is surrounded by dramatic scenery, ranging from lush jungle to the green peaks of the enveloping mountains. Before the revolution, it was also home to the Laotian royal family, but during the years following the civil war – and the abolition of the royal family – the town was all but forgotten. Ironically, it was this period of neglect that helped preserve it. There are many places around the globe where Communism has 'pickled' the architecture – perhaps more out of disinterest than concern – and Luang Prabang is a stellar example of this.

The Apsara, Ivan's hotel, is in a converted former warehouse on the banks of the mighty Mekong. It is named after the carved dancing maidens that adorn the temple walls of Angkor Wat in neighbouring Cambodia. The choice of name is appropriate: the hotel seduces you with its extraordinary setting and laid-back, distinctively Asian style. The guest rooms upstairs have high ceilings and balconies that look out over the famous river. Downstairs,

the old storerooms have been converted into an atmospheric bar, a cosy living area and an intimate restaurant.

After settling in at the hotel, I joined an English-speaking local I'd met on the flight for a coffee in the main street of Luang Prabang, which is packed with cafés, boulangeries and boutiques displaying a heady mix of French and Asian influences. It's easy to understand the attraction of this town for tourists. It offers a taste of the region's extraordinary history in idyllic, unspoiled surroundings, and it is small enough that you can walk everywhere. On an elegant veranda with wicker tables, I tucked into a café au lait and a local cake and took the opportunity to ask my new aquaintance about something that I had noticed on the flight over. Did he know why there were so many gay couples on the plane from Bangkok? Without a hint of irony, he smiled and said, 'It's because of the clubs. There are three gay nightclubs in town.'

'Seems strange for such a small place,' I said. 'Why so many?'

'Because of the monks!' he replied.

The monks? 'What do monks have to do with the number of gay nightclubs in this town?' I asked.

'When they have finished their prayers and their chores and their meditation', he explained, 'the monks go to bed. But some sneak out of their monasteries in the early hours, in their "civvies", to party in the clubs.'

Apparently no one notices or cares very much as long as they are back in time for the dawn ritual.

This may seem surprising behaviour for monks, but Buddhism doesn't preach morality in the same way that Western religions do. The basic underlying tenet of the faith is that you can do as you like, so long as it doesn't hurt anybody or anything else.

On Ivan's advice, I learned that the place to be in Luang Prabang, just before dawn, is on the streets, in time to catch the start of a fascinating ritual: the daily collection of alms. The monks walk around town in single file with their begging bowls to collect enough rice to eat. They receive only a few grains each from the devout followers who bring their pots of cooked rice to give to the thousands of monks, so it takes quite a while before they have enough to fill their bowls even partially. Once their bowls are full enough, they walk back, still in single file, to their monasteries. In this way, the monks have to work for their meagre meal, which becomes an exercise in humility and an opportunity for the faithful to participate in a public act of kindness. I was there on my first morning with my camera to document the whole parade, and it was, as promised, an absorbing spectacle. I tried very hard to spot the monks who might have just left the nightclubs, but to no avail. So: if you want to know how to party all night long without anyone knowing, ask a monk in Luang Prabang

And my passport, the one in two pieces?

There was a girl at the reception desk of the Apsara who was a whizz with Scotch tape. She taped my data page back into the passport, which lasted, amazingly, until it expired four years later.

PROVENCE
FRANCE
CHÂTEAU DE MASSILIAN

*Fields of sunflowers and lavender and a
12th-century castle distinguish a quiet corner
of the French countryside immortalized
by Cézanne and van Gogh*

Surrounded by blazingly bright fields of yellow sunflowers and contrasting expanses of lavender, Château de Massillan is a charismatic blend of historic grandeur, rustic charm and splendid isolation.

It's everything you might hope for in France: a 12th-century castle complete with crenellated walls and watchtowers surrounded by the Provençal landscape immortalized in paintings and books. It's the kind of place that might have served as inspiration for van Gogh or Cézanne.

Inside, however, the château is refreshingly contemporary in an original, eclectic way. You won't find any Souleiado Indian-style printed cottons, baskets of potpourri or potted plants in mustard-coloured faïence – the decorative details that we have come to associate with Provence. Instead, the contemporary style of the interior is complemented by select antiques, clean, minimalist furniture upholstered in pale linen, all-white industrial-chic bathrooms with Chinese bamboo ladders for hanging towels, and big empty spaces that the designer has resisted any temptation to fill up. If Coco Chanel had owned a place in Provence, it might have looked like this.

Château de Massillan is rustic enough to give you the flavour and ambience of the area, yet modern enough to function as a great place to chill. It offers a perfect combination of the seductive natural beauty of Provence and a sophisticated style that dares to break away from the desire to be conspicuously 'authentic'. This is a great place to get away from work and city life, and let your mind breathe.

The exotically named Birgit Israel, a German-born, London-based designer, is the woman behind it all. Appropriately, there's a touch of Coco Chanel about her. She is fiercely independent, driven and secure in her own sense of style. She loves antiques and is an avid flea-market hunter, although she only displays her finds selectively, as she understands that the most effective visual tool is contrast: if you really want to notice a spectacular antique chandelier, it is best to hang it in a largely empty space. Her signature style is not limited to interiors. She also operates two of the most successful recycled fashion shops in London. Her speciality is her keen ability to edit and mix from disparate, unexpected sources – vintage Chanel with cutting-edge Japanese labels, for example – a quality that also shines through at Château de Massillan.

Château de Massillan is ideal for the traveller who is familiar enough with Provence to recognize where its enduring attractions lie – in its natural beauty, its history and the quality of its daily life. In the scaring midday heat of summer, the bustling towns with their cafés, restaurants and ancient Roman monuments, coupled with the permanently cerulean sky, the jagged rocky peaks of the surrounding Alpilles mountains and the incessant clicking of the cicadas make this area an excitingly exotic place to be.

Better still, Château de Massillan is in the Vaucluse, a corner of Provence that has not been exploited and overdeveloped like the Luberon. The château lies north of Avignon, near Orange, a

town famed for a magnificent Roman amphitheatre and triumphal arch that have survived almost intact. The area around Orange is quiet because most fans of Provence head south when they get to Avignon, so you don't need to worry about groups of tourists with big cameras looking for Peter Mayle's house or Alain Ducasse's latest restaurant. There's no need for the latter, as the château itself has a superb restaurant, offering seasonal French cuisine as fresh and contemporary in presentation as the hotel's interior.

I knew of Birgit Israel's style because I have admired her design shops for many years. The opportunity to visit and photograph her château coincided nicely with the planned filming of a *HIP Hotels* television pilot for Discovery Channel. Why not do both at the same time?

So in the end a Washington DC-based company (Discovery) set out to work on a pilot with a London-based author (me) and an Australian-based crew and director in France. Talk about a global village. We met up on Île de Ré on the Atlantic coast of France and drove in two cars to Provence. Why we didn't just meet in Provence is something I never quite figured out. Maybe it was so they could get footage of us on the road; if that was indeed the case, we certainly gave them plenty of material because we got very lost trying to find Château de Massillan.

After a day in the car we arrived. The director and the Discovery Channel guy immediately announced that we were going to the

Roman theatre to see an extravagant costume drama. They asked whether this was the kind of thing I would normally do. 'Probably not!' I replied. But we went anyway. It was interesting and atmospheric, but sitting on a stone slab for more than two hours was not. Either Romans had incredible tolerance for discomfort or they had much shorter theatrical productions than the one we saw.

The next day I had planned to start photographing Château de Massillan, but my companions had other ideas. We were all going to the winery of Châteauneuf-du-Pape, they declared. 'Is that something you would normally do?' they asked. 'Probably not!' was my answer. And off we went. I did enjoy the story behind the name of the winery, which literally translates as 'the new castle of the Pope'. In the 14th century the papacy was relocated to Avignon and the winery is located right next to the ruin of what was once the Pope's new castle. That's the part I liked – the history. Wandering around a cellar tasting this and that, when the weather was amazing outside and we could have been doing some real exploring, was not.

Much to my surprise, the Discovery pilot tested very well. Maybe the audience could sense the tension between me and the crew and director, or maybe they thought it was funny that I kept having to do things that I would not normally do. Then it dawned on me that the 'misfits on the road' scenario created a strangely watchable dynamic because, when it comes to travel, it's the things that go wrong that you remember most.

All the châteaux of France are spectacular simply due to their history, scale and setting but Château de Massillan also offers the magic ingredients of sunshine and warmth for most of the year. The interiors are stunning and unexpected, but the outside areas are where you will spend most of your time.

Ancient and classic on the outside, pared-down and quirky on the inside, it's a decorative combination that gives Château de Massillan contemporary relevance. Jewelry designer Birgit Israel's signature style transforms this historic stone pile into the setting for a modern lifestyle we can all relate to.

PORTOFINO
ITALY

ALBERGO DA GIOVANNI

*A 16th-century monastery situated on the water's edge
and an Italian 'Mama' whose family has been
cooking here for 400 years, in a hidden cove
just around the corner from Portofino*

Of all the former fishing villages in Italy that have morphed into highly desirable destinations for the super-rich with their super-yachts, Portofino is surely one of the most spectacular. Set against a backdrop of imposing mountains, nestled into a natural fold of forest-clad granite cliffs, Portofino has that rare blend of unspoiled natural beauty, sophisticated manmade luxury and conspicuous consumption. Louis Vuitton boutiques, gold bikinis, cafés that charge in the double digits for a coffee, towering luxury boats and legendary grand hotels such as Splendido all coexist in a small, charming seaside town that was once part of the city-state of Genoa. It's a dream to stay here but it can be a nightmare for your wallet.

Luckily, this is Italy, where you can always count on the Catholic Church to come to the rescue. Twenty minutes by boat from Portofino lies the monastery of San Fruttuoso – a place that is much more exotic than Portofino and much more affordable. Byzantine in its foundation, it was inhabited by Benedictine monks until the 1500s. Its location was chosen as the ideal spot to hide the relics of the martyr Fruttuoso from marauding Saracen pirates. The imposing tower that flanks the structure was built in 1562 by the famous Genocse general Andrea Doria, who is buried at the monastery.

Tucked into a fold in the near-vertical slopes of the southern Alpine ridge that cascades into the Mediterranean, the monastery cannot be seen from the sea, nor can it be reached by land. The only way to get to San Fruttuoso is by boat. Today a regular service from Portofino and Camogli brings hundreds of day-trippers wanting to swim, sunbathe and eat.

Hospitality is the new *raison d'être* of this hidden gem. Centuries ago entrepreneur Lorenzo Bozzo set up a trattoria to cater to the pilgrims visiting the tomb of Andrea Doria and, remarkably, the restaurant is still operated by the same family. Bozzo's son was called Giovanni and his name became permanently associated with the building. Towards the end of the 16th century, after the last of the monks had gone, the Bozzo family was given permission to divide the cloister into private lodgings and, for the next four centuries, they were the primary residents of this inaccessible cove. They made a meagre living from the sea until the second half of the 20th century when tourism began to develop as a much more lucrative option.

On the surface, there appears to be nowhere for visitors to stay. After the last ferry has departed, San Fruttuoso returns to its monastic character – calm, quiet, serene – the perfect ambience to take in the sheer beauty of the place. If you ignore the few remaining boats, it is easy to imagine the Benedictine monks of old going about their day-to-day lives here in splendid isolation. There's a touch of Umberto Eco's *The Name of the Rose* about the place, and like the monastery in Eco's book, San Fruttuoso, too, has a secret. There is a way you can stay here overnight and it does not involve pledging your life to God. You just have to know the right person.

You will find her in the kitchen of Albergo da Giovanni restaurant, cooking. She also happens to be the proprietor and is a distant descendant of the original Bozzo. Signora Bozzo's restaurant is classic Italian: noisy and charmingly disorganized. In the midst of all the yelling, cajoling and singing, it seemed strange to ask about my reservation as she distractedly stirred a huge pot while wiping her brow with her apron. But she knew all about it. Next to her pots and pans she had a pegboard with keys. Throwing a set to me, she gestured to someone to show me my room. Signora Bozzo has a dozen rooms that are available to let. They are not luxurious but they do have a shower and a bidet (strangely, the toilet is down the hall) and a view that even the most expensive hotel in Portofino (and that's saying something) would be hard-pressed to match.

The rooms are not part of the monastery, so they are not former monastic cells, but neither could they be classified as suites. They simply offer a private space in a magical location that from early evening to early morning gives you the monastery, the turquoise-coloured cove, the watchtower and the pebble beach all to yourself. The rooms are basic, though not small, and furnished in such an eccentric manner that you could imagine an avant-garde fashion label shooting its next catalogue in them. Mine had two different floral wallpapers on three different walls and faux-brick paper on the fourth, all of which contrasted bizarrely with the florals and geometrics of the curtains and the voiles.

The windows of my room opened onto a view of the tiny turquoise bay. Directly in my line of sight was a small rowboat that had a hand-painted sign on it: 'Available for hire and private excursions'. It made me smile. Who, here in the Italian capital of mega-yachts, would hire an old wooden rowboat? The next day I had my answer: me! I had just missed the last ferry of the afternoon and, much as I would have loved to stay another night, I had to get back to Portofino and back on the road. With no road access from San Fruttuoso – not even a rudimentary donkey trail or a path that might be used by pedestrians willing to make the hike – I was stuck. The only way back to Portofino was to hire the rowboat and its captain.

It was a journey that bordered on the bizarre. There must have been a storm somewhere out in the Mediterranean. In contrast to the balmy calm of the day I when arrived, the sea was running an impressive swell that was dumping big waves onto San Fruttuoso's pebble beach. The captain of my rowboat (hard to say with a straight face) met me at the dock. I explained that I really needed to get to Portofino and he nodded with a crinkle of the brow, a sweep of the arms and a wicked wink that said 'Let's go…if you're game!'

The quickest route was to stick closely to the rocky coast. But the captain and I obviously had very different ideas about the meaning of 'closely'. The sheer walls of granite that characterize this part of the Italian coast are breathtakingly beautiful but that doesn't mean I wanted to see them at point-blank range. Our little boat regularly

Tucked into a cove hidden from view, the quiet, isolated former Franciscan
monastery of San Fruttuoso is a startling surprise, considering its close proximity
to the wealthy, fashionable tourist destination of Portofino. The fact that it is still
only accessible by boat makes it irresistibly compelling; the fact (unbeknownst
to almost everyone) that you can stay the night makes it priceless.

disappeared into the waves and then the massive swell would pick up the vessel and send it rushing straight at the vertical walls of beautiful, glistening granite. I braced myself for impact, expecting our little craft to be splintered into a thousand pieces as it hurled towards the imposing rockface, but every time, at what seemed to be the very last second, the wave, bouncing off the solid walls, would pick up the boat and send us surfing back out again. The captain seemed to think it was great fun. He was smiling and singing and whooping

every time we almost got crushed against the rocks. I think he had done this before. Either that or he was completely insane. I, on the other hand, was thinking only about the short lifespan of my camera and the niggling question of how, in super-sophisticated Portofino, I had somehow managed to land myself in an Italian version of *Moby Dick*.

Eventually we arrived in Portofino and I can honestly say that I have never looked forward so much to being ripped off in a café.

SIWA
EGYPT
SHALI LODGE

Temples, oracles and legends in an ancient
date-palm oasis, right in the middle
of the Sahara desert

Rustic, ethnic, authentic: plenty of desirable adjectives ending in 'ic' apply to Shali Lodge – including 'economic'. This small hidden gem boasts an irresistible combination of unusual textures, colours and earthly charm, and Is situated In a town in the heart of the Sahara that has enjoyed mythic status since 2,000 years before the birth of Christ. If you want to experience something of the Egypt of antiquity, without hordes of sunburned, sandal-wearing tourists, then Shali Lodge in Siwa is for you.

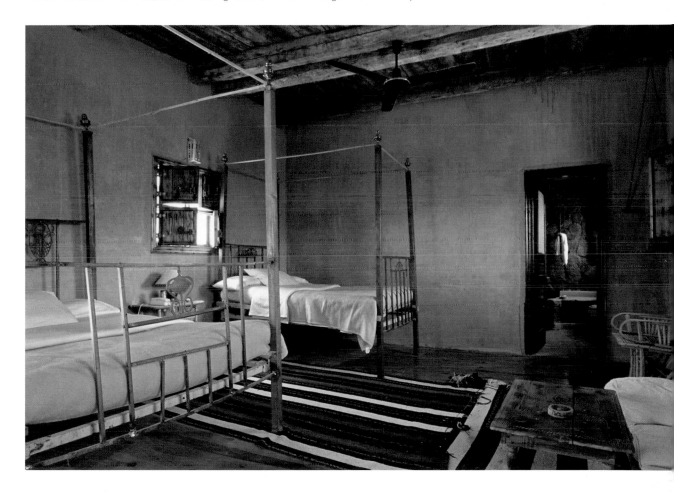

S iwa is a mythic place. Hardly anyone has ever heard of it and even fewer have been there, yet this tiny oasis, hidden in a vast sea of sand in the middle of the Sahara desert, was famous long before the birth of Christ. This was where Pharaoh Ahmose II (570–526 BC) decided to build the temple of the oracle of the god Amun and where, two hundred years later, Alexander the Great – who is said to have followed a flock of birds across the desert – came to consult the same oracle: to ask if it was true that he was half-man, half-god. He got the answer he wanted (yes, he was half-god, the son of Amun) and off he went to conquer half the world.

Siwa is the stuff of legend, but since at least 3000 BC it has also been famous for its dates. More than a million date palms surround this tiny town on the banks of an enormous lake. It sounds improbable – a vast stretch of water interrupting a seemingly infinite expanse of sand, but it's not a mirage; it's an extraordinary freak of nature. Siwa sits on top of an immense underground reservoir. The water that has gradually seeped to the surface to create the lake continues to irrigate the palm trees and olive trees that have made Siwa famous since antiquity.

This has to be one of the most remote and exotic places on the planet. It's a fourteen-hour drive to Siwa from Cairo. First you head north to Alexandria, then west along the Mediterranean until you're not far from the border with Libya, then you turn south and drive four more hours through the largest sand deposit on earth. If you have

seen the opening scenes of *The English Patient*, you'll get the idea.

I was travelling with a French television crew and I admit we cheated: we flew. It was in a Beechcraft King Air, a prop-jet – not the largest plane, but very reliable. We took off from Cairo, headed west, and within minutes were over an endless expanse of sand. It looked hot and unforgiving, but in the plane our teeth were chattering. There was no heating in the cabin and the temperature had very quickly dipped below zero. We (the French crew and myself) were of course dressed for the Sahara: shorts, T-shirts and sandals – not a sweater, scarf or jacket between us. We should have noticed that the pilots were wearing thick *Top Gun*-style jackets when we took off. The flight was just under an hour and it was the coldest 45 minutes of my life. The worst part when you get really cold is the urge to pee. But there were no facilities available because they had used the one and only cubicle for our luggage (film crews have lots of gear). When we finally landed at a military airbase just outside Siwa it took a while for the feeling to return in my toes. We must have appeared very odd to the people who met us at the plane, hobbling awkwardly on the tarmac with tortured looks on our faces.

From that point on, the French crew believed they were cursed. The more secret tombs we visited, and the more legendary ancient temples we filmed and photographed, the more anxious they became – we were obviously angering the spirits. By the second night they had decided to sleep in the same room because they

were having the same vivid nightmare of being assaulted by a creature that was half-man, half-ram (the form, according to Herodutus, taken by Amun). The producer, a veteran journalist who had reported from many war zones, was completely spooked. I, on the other hand, slept very well.

It was here, in this unspoiled, slightly unsettling desert outpost, that Dr Mounir, a professor at the University of Cairo, chose to build a retreat that would serve as a shining example of minimal environmental impact and eco-friendly sustainability. His project, Adrère Amellal, has become almost as much of a legend as the place itself. The entire lakeside compound, which is sizeable, was built from mud and salt. The mud was compressed to make building blocks and the salt, which had been baking in the Sahara sun for thousands of years, was cut into big slabs and used for the floors and, in some cases, even for opaque windows. Adrère Amellal has no telecommunications or electricity, and at night all the rooms and public spaces are lit with an abundance of beeswax candles. The food, in line with the retreat's eco-friendly approach, comes from the kitchen garden. It may well sound primitive, but in fact the absence of modern luxuries and the pared-down purity of the experience make this place different, exciting and wonderfully captivating.

It's not cheap, however. Like most handmade, one-off creations, Adrère Amellal comes at a price and, although it is without doubt worth every penny, it simply will not suit everyone's budget. But the tenacious Dr Mounir has thought of that too. He wants to share his vision of an eco-friendly, sustainable future with as many people as possible and for that reason he has built a smaller and more affordable version on the other side of town. It is called Shali Lodge and is similar in style to Adrère Amellal. One big difference between the two is location: whereas Adrère Amellal sits under a pale cliff at the very edge of the lake, Shali Lodge is right in town. Although you don't get the view of the lake, you do get the charm of this fascinating village.

Aesthetically Mounir has stuck to the same formula: mud-brick walls and floors made of salt or stone. Even the furniture is made exclusively from the fronds that fall naturally from the multitude of date palms, an almost infinite source of materials.

Shali is a beautiful and inspirational place, but the oasis remains the main attraction in Siwa. This is a world of forgotten tombs and abandoned temples in a town that did not have a bank until Dr Mounir built one and that still counts more donkeys than cars. The surrounding area is ripe for adventure. A must is a trip by four-wheel-drive through the Sahara, crossing a landscape of unending monumental sand dunes. It's a rollercoaster ride with a few strange extras – for example, unexpected stops for swimming in cold-water lakes, bang in the middle of all this heat and sand (something that, apparently, also attracted British troops during the Second World War when, taking a break from fighting Rommel's men, they scandalized the locals by skinny dipping).

The most mesmerizing feature of all, however, is the silence. We are so accustomed to noise that we have forgotten how impressive (and scary) total silence can be (just ask the French film crew). It's like total darkness. And both can be experienced in Siwa.

It has been many years since my Siwa adventure, yet every time I set foot in a grocery store in Paris that is run by an Algerian, Tunisian, Moroccan or Egyptian, they stop and say, 'Ahhh! C'est vous, le mec de Siwa.' (It's you, the guy from Siwa.) So perhaps the film crew was right: there are strange forces at work. Or maybe it's just because of the re-runs on prime-time French television.

CAP FERRET
FRANCE
LA MAISON DU BASSIN

Rustic charm, oyster beds, brilliant food and
massive sand dunes in an little-known corner
of France's south-west coast

Cap Ferret, like nearby Île de Ré, is a secret that those crafty Parisians have kept to themselves. Heard of it? Everybody thinks they have, but that's only because it sounds so much like Cap Ferrat – as in St-Jean-Cap-Ferrat. But Cap Ferret and Cap Ferrat are two completely different places.

Cap Ferrat is on the French Riviera. It is horribly expensive, and very close to Monte Carlo (which, most Parisians will agree, is not a good thing) and counts more Russian (very wealthy Russian) than French residents. Cap Ferret, by contrast, is on the south-west coast of France, on the Bassin d'Arcachon. It is wild and unspoilt and boasts some of the highest sand dunes in Europe. The population is close to 100 per cent French. Rather than drawing the wealthy international yachting crowd, Cap Ferret's reputation for sophisticated simplicity attracts people who want to sail small boats, live in rustic wooden houses, enjoy wild beaches and eat oysters.

My first experience of Cap Ferret was with a French television personality, Cendrine Dominguez, who is something of a younger Gallic version of Martha Stewart. We were working on a coffee-table book about houses in different regions of France. One of the chapters focused on the traditional houses of Cap Ferret: the wooden beach shacks that are as stylistically distinctive as the clapboard cottages of Cape Cod. This charmingly rustic architecture owes its origins to the unique wooden structures built on stilts in the area's tidal basins. These rugged *cabanes de gardian*, which were introduced

in the Napoleonic era to protect the local oyster beds from thieves, have inspired the wooden vacation homes that are now so sought after by Parisians. They are usually two-storey structures with a veranda that wraps around the ground floor and an open-plan layout that is almost loft-like in its spaciousness.

Although it was only April when I visited, I remember it being warm and sunny. Cap Ferret is very close to the Basque coast of Spain, so the summer starts earlier than coastal regions further north, such as Normandy and Brittany. People were already heading to the beach when we arrived. It was also oyster season, so we had an opportunity to experience the real culinary culture of Cap Ferret. The owner of the house we had been photographing had invited me and Cendrine for a typical local lunch. The table was set outdoors, with a plain linen tablecloth and a few bottles of white wine. The oysters arrived on a massive round platter the size of a small table, set on a raised metal stand. There was a basket of baguettes, a green salad with tomatoes and olive oil, a big slab of butter and some lemons. Nothing else. That day I ate more oysters than I would normally eat in a year. To be perfectly honest, I'm surprised that I enjoyed it. Normally six oysters will do for me as a starter, but here the oysters are both the starter and the main course.

It was because of Cendrine – once the star of a very strange French gameshow called *Fort Boyard* (which was set, bizarrely, in an abandoned maritime prison on a rocky island in the Atlantic)

and then the host of a popular interior design programme called *La Maison de Cendrine* – that I discovered La Maison du Bassin. I needed somewhere to stay for the duration of the shoot and La Maison du Bassin turned out to be *the* place. With only seven guest rooms, this hidden gem is a secret within a secret: a place people prefer to keep to themselves, tucked away in a place they prefer to keep to themselves. And for good reason. Not only is it disarmingly charming and pretty in a natural and unpretentious way, but it also happens to be one of the best spots to eat in the whole of Cap Ferret. The seafood is amazing and the desserts can compete with the best patisseries in Paris. Plus, it's on the beach (well, almost) and boasts not only a view of the sea and but also a panorama of the nearby oyster beds with their charming wooden *cabanes de gardian*.

Many people who know La Maison du Bassin forget it is a hotel because it is so popular as a place to drink and eat. The advantage you have as outsider is that most Parisians who frequent Cap Ferret have their own vacation houses, so the hotel is not as heavily booked as one might imagine. Aesthetically, the interior combines the rustic charm of a rugged seaside location with the soft feminine flair of a typically French shabby-chic interior. It's cosy but not overly so. It doesn't bombard you with cushions and pot-pourri, and it has enough polished dark wood to maintain its maritime dignity.

The best part of La Maison du Bassin is that the atmosphere is as French as it gets. It's the kind of place that would make an ideal setting for a French farce. The protagonists – an apparently perfect family consisting of a conservative, self-sacrificing husband who is a moral pillar of society, his immaculately groomed wife who is not only a wonderful mother but also a Cordon Bleu cook, and their impeccably behaved children dressed in Bonpoint (a ridiculously expensive Parisian label that specializes in cashmere for children) – go there every year *en vacances*. And then, over the summer, the truth slowly unravels in ruthlessly devilish fashion: the husband has been having an affair with the children's nanny, the kids are smoking pot on the beach and the wife has been having 'extra lessons' with her daughter's tennis instructor boyfriend, and so on.

Ahhh, the French: behind the joys of uncomplicated simplicity lies complex intrigue. That's why the world is so attracted to this country. Did you honestly think it was just the weather and the food?

With its natural beauty, unaffected and effortless style and fabulous food – the holy trinity of French hospitality – as well as the fact that this remarkable retreat is also affordable and virtually unknown on the tourist circuit, it's easy to understand why the French are so keen to keep Cap Ferret a secret.

KOH SAMUI
THAILAND
MUANG KULAYPAN

*Japanese beds, Thai dance and fearless
modernity on a Koh Samui beach*

Koh Samui could hardly be described as new or undiscovered. You only have to walk down the main street of Chaweng, with its impressive array of open-air restaurants, to understand that this island has embraced tourism without reservation. In addition to the seemingly unlimited choice of cuisine, almost every major hotel brand has opened an outpost here, including Six Senses, Four Seasons and W, to name a few. It's all attractively designed and luxuriously presented, but it's not distinctively Thai.

Muang Kulaypan is different. It's not just in the amazing details: the Japanese-inspired bedrooms with wooden floors and platform beds, the dark bathrooms with sinks set into great slabs of tree trunk, the black swimming pool or the minimalist white beach lounges. There's something innately unusual about Muang Kulaypan that goes beyond design features. Its style is modern for sure but, more importantly, its soul is bohemian. The restaurant, for instance, consists of a series of thatched-roof pagodas built in the indigenous style on the grass adjacent to the beach. Sitting cross-legged on ikat cushions, you eat authentic local food while watching a polished and highly regarded performance of traditional Thai dance.

This is not design simply for the sake of being different, but design intended to have genuine cultural relevance. The hotel preserves the traditions of Thailand not only in its appearance but also in its dedication to dance, one of the most enduring Thai art forms.

By developing and sustaining a well-respected school of traditional dance on the premises, Muang Kulaypan is able to introduce the traveller to genuine Thai culture without lowering standards or turning it into a Disney version of Old Siam. It's all about including a bit of culture with your fix of tropical sun, sea and sand. As a guest at Muang Kulaypan, you get to spend plenty of time in the sun, but because of the way this hotel is put together, you cannot help but be drawn into the local customs.

Even the hotel's name reflects its commitment to traditional culture. Considering that Thai dance is at the heart of the Muang Kulaypan experience, it's appropriate that the name relates to a traditional dance. Muang Kulaypan was an ancient city on Java where a prince named Inao (Inu Panyee Karatapati) had a reputation as a great warrior and lover. The story of his romance with the beautiful Princess Budsaba travelled from Java to Thailand, where it inspired a dance that became a favourite at the Thai royal court.

Cultural resonance, a regard for history and tradition, a bohemian sense of art and design: these are not the values usually associated with a resort hotel on a beach, but it makes more sense when you consider that both the owner and the designer are Thai graduates of the École Nationale Supérieure des Beaux-Arts in Paris, a school that promotes integrity, authenticity and longevity as well as creativity, lessons that clearly have been put into practice at Muang Kulaypan. In a way, the hotel is itself like an art installation, and as a guest you become part of something that changes and evolves. This makes Muang Kulaypan refreshingly different from most hotels, which tend to work hard at removing any element of change or risk from their guests' experience.

When I was there, a baby elephant named Dunah had become part of the family. He ran around on the grass next to the stylish all-black swimming pool, played with the guests on the beach, and, when it was time for his ritual daily bath in the sea, all the guests would turn up to watch the rotund little rascal frolic. It was hard to imagine that just one year earlier he had been a tiny, scared thing, abused on the streets of Bangkok. But the next time I was there, he was gone. He had grown up, and it was time for him to join other mature elephants. I liked the fact that the hotel didn't go out and get another baby elephant. It would have cheapened the memory of Dunah, and it would have spoiled the gesture of genuine kindness that he represented. He had been at Muang Kulaypan because he needed help – not to entertain the guests. The fact that he did entertain everyone while he was there was a very welcome but temporary bonus.

Muang Kulaypan is an oasis of authenticity and cultural integrity on a island that sometimes seems to take its own natural beauty for granted. Sure, the white beaches and turquoise waters are stunning, but there is much more on offer here. All you need is a boat.

About an hour south of Koh Samui is a clump of islands that are practically uninhabited and offer a plethora of opportunities for adventure. Sheer cliffs surround deep lagoons where you can step off the boat straight onto the jagged ledges of a vertical rock face and test your climbing skills. If your feet slip, you simply fall into the deep, clear turquoise waters of the lagoon

For fans of diving and snorkelling, there are plenty of magical spots in the area. One that struck me in particular is a tiny remote island (so tiny and remote that I never learned its name) surrounded by sandbars that you can only get to by snorkelling. The island features a small ancient temple that is guarded by a pack of dogs. The noise they make as you try to approach by stealth (which is pointless, considering that snorkelling is not exactly stealthy) is intimidating, and the second you touch the beach and attempt to stand up they run at you in a pack, barking and snarling so loudly that you want to dive straight back in and swim away. But when they get close enough to touch, it's clear that they are only starved of attention, and have learned to associate snorkellers with fun…and feeding time. You can't expect the dogs to be able to tell one snorkeller from another.

Truth be known, all the things that make Thailand so special are still there for the picking on and around Koh Samui; you just have to know where to look. And Muang Kulaypan is a good place to start.

Koh Samui, sometimes called 'the Maui of Thailand', is far less touristy and developed than Phuket, while it still ticks all the usual boxes: turquoise water, white-sand beaches and lots of sun. But for those who want culture and originality as well as spectacular beaches, the modern, quirky Muang Kulaypan delivers on all fronts, offering an experience that is at once refreshingly different and yet the most distinctively Thai of all the resorts on the island.

Thai culture is introduced in the most refined manner at Muang Kulaypan. Its restaurant, for example, serves traditional Thai food to guests seated in raised, thatched pavilions that overlook an outdoor theatre, which features polished nightly performances of traditional Thai dance by the members of the famous and widely respected school located on the premises.

LUANG PRABANG
LAOS
SATRI HOUSE

Romantic ambience and French colonial
style in the best-preserved town in all
of South East Asia

Hidden in the jungle beside a bend in the mighty Mekong River is Luang Prabang, a tiny
town that plays host to hundreds of Buddhist monks and magnificent, well-preseved remnants
of the French Indochine, Satri House provides a glimpse into the exotic glamour of colonial
life in a forgotten corner of South East Asia.

Remember Ivan? The owner of the Apsara in Luang Prabang (page 20)? His girlfriend, Lamphoune Voravongsa, also has a hotel in this splendid UNESCO World Heritage-listed town.

Whereas the Apsara is in a converted warehouse on the banks of the Mekong River, Lamphoune's place, Satri House, is an intact French colonial mansion on the outskirts of town. It is more decorative and refined than Ivan's place and completely authentic in a different way, offering insight into how the colonial French lived when this landlocked Buddhist nation was briefly part of the Indochine. Surrounded by lush gardens, it is an elegantly isolated place to stay, yet you are only a few minutes' walk from town.

With its terracotta-tiled floors, shuttered windows and neoclassical detailing, the building looks like it could be the set of the film *Indochine*. The guest rooms are spacious, with high ceilings, polished timber floors, four-poster beds and verandas or balconies that open out into the lush green of the surrounding jungle. It's the kind of hotel that is perfect for a long stay: roomy and luxurious, with a splendid swimming pool and a completely private garden.

The name Satri means 'house of women', which is appropriate not only because the hotel is owned and operated by a woman, something still unusual in Laos, but also because the interior ambience is distinctively feminine. From the decorative fabrics (Laotian raw silk and linen) to the Chinese, Vietnamese and Thai antiques, there is a pervasive sensuousness that reflects a woman's touch. Judging

from the easy, effortless colonial style of the interior, I wasn't surprised to learn that Lamphoune had been educated in France and had lived in Paris before returning to Laos. It had never been her intention to become a hotelier, but when she was invited to this house for dinner by a client (she was at the time in the jewelry and fabric business, based in Vientiane) who mentioned that the house was for sale, she decided she had to have it.

Whereas Ivan taught me a lot about Luang Prabang's monks, Lamphoune showed me new and authentic ways to experience this extraordinary place. On my second day in town – the day I first saw the monks walk around town collecting alms – the three of us (Ivan, Lamphoune and myself) went for lunch in a place that looked like a chicken farm. A rustic chicken farm. As roosters and hens ran around noisily, occasionally chased by the staff, we were served an extraordinary chicken dish in the shade of a small thatched veranda. I told Ivan and Lamphoune that I loved places like this – places that are not only surprising, unusual and authentic, but also encourage you to try something new.

Lamphoune said that if I really wanted to try something new and authentic, I should come out dancing with them in a real Laotian nightclub. I remembered the stories I'd heard about the monks, and finally curiosity got the better of me, so we arranged to go out that night. Ivan picked us up in his car and we drove along the town's jungle-fringed streets until we came to a building that I would never

have imagined had anything to do with Luang Prabang, let alone its nightlife. The huge concrete structure, with its big car park, looked like a bingo hall in New Jersey. The music was loud, and there were hundreds of people inside the vintage Communist-era interior of what, I learned, had originally been built as a Scout hall. The decor consisted of little more than a collection of chairs and round tables – with tablecloths and the lace doilies that all Communist regimes seem to be so fond of – arranged with military precision around a massive dance floor. It wasn't pretty, but it did have a great *Footloose* vibe.

A lot of people were nervously standing around the dance floor, which was all but empty, though not for long. The band kicked in with what sounded like vintage Asian disco – with a heavy but consistent bass beat and a Laotian lady whispering pillow talk into the microphone – and suddenly everyone rushed onto the dance floor, including Lamphoune. Within a matter of seconds, they had organized themselves into a series of neat straight rows and, as if on cue, started to line-dance.

It was a unique cultural phenomenon, and I wouldn't have missed it for the world. Take the hip-swaying of Hawaiian hula, combine it with the bird-like head movements and elegant hand extensions of traditional Thai dance, throw in the rhythmic stomping, jumping

and kicking of American country-western, and you have the magic of Laotian line dancing. I could have watched it all night but Lamphoune had other ideas. After her first few solo sessions, she dragged Ivan and me onto the floor. Ivan was okay because he had tried it before; I, on the other hand, looked like Mr Bean. Although I didn't exactly glide through the moves, I loved the music and the ambience and the strange but infectious vibe and I was happy I had come. Those Laotians certainly knew how to party...with dignity!

Who would have thought that so much would be happening in a sleepy little colonial town on the banks of the Mekong River? Chicken-chasing, line-dancing, partying until dawn with Buddhist monks: Luang Prabang is definitely the wildcard in South East Asia, a sort of New Orleans of Indochina.

When I look back to the start of my journey, forgetting the unfortunate incident with the ornately costumed colonel (see page 20), I honestly had few expectations and had pegged Luang Prabang as a place more for seeing than for doing. And that's the fun of travel, isn't it? Places will surprise you; people will surprise you and you can never know what they're like until you've been there yourself.

Selfishly, I hope Luang Prabang doesn't catch on with too many people. This is one place I would hate to see change.

Satri House is surrounded by the dense jungle that typifies the local landscape. Verdant leaves, vines and palm fronds constantly fight their way into the building. Unlike most luxury resorts, which go to a lot of effort to remove any sense of wilderness from the vegetation, Satri House proudly remains a splendid French colonial house that looks as if it's about to be swallowed up by the jungle.

Outside it's all lush and green; inside it's an ethnic play on contemporary style. There are touches of Laotian influence but the interiors mainly reflect the individual taste of the proprietor, who grew up in France and studied in Paris before returning to her native Laos.

GOA
INDIA
FORT TIRACOL

*A pared-down Portuguese colonial fort
surrounded by sweeping beaches
and swaying palms*

Goa is the Brazil of India. With its beautiful beaches and famously laid-back lifestyle, it has been a magnet for hedonistic hippies and beach bums for decades. Peace and love seem so much more attainable when you are on a tropical coast surrounded by white sand and palm trees; even more so when it's affordable and comes with a Portuguese-style vibe. But nowadays it's not just the hippies who flock to India's west coast. Newly affluent Indians are also developing a taste for Goan-style beach life. The legacy left by Goa's Portuguese colonizers goes beyond buildings and last names: in Goa, as in Brazil, they really know how to party!

A few years ago I stayed at a place in Goa that has become especially famous for its partying: the beautiful hotel Nilaya Hermitage. Its owners, Hari and Claudia Sebir, have a rare talent for combining great aesthetics, a laid-back atmosphere and serious partying in exactly the right proportions. When they told me about Fort Tiracol Heritage Hotel, in an old Portuguese fort that they had recently renovated in the north of Goa, I had to go. A car was ready to take me, but first I had to stay for dinner. Hari and Claudia insisted. I should have left as soon as we finished dinner, but we were having such a good time that I stayed for some after-dinner drinks. Although it was past midnight by the time I got into the car, my hosts, who very kindly waved me off, assured me it was better this way: less traffic and fewer distractions (for the driver – not for me!).

We drove north to the very tip of Goa where it almost touches the neighbouring state of Maharashtra, separated only by the powerful Terekhol River. As my hosts had predicted, the road was dead quiet and very dark, like a tree-lined tunnel. I drifted off to sleep on the back seat and woke only when the reassuringly regular bumps in the road stopped. I looked at my watch: 2 AM.

'Have we arrived?' I asked the driver. 'No sir,' he replied, 'We are waiting for the ferry.' 'What ferry?' I asked, still half asleep. 'The ferry on the other side of the river,' he answered. 'When will it be here?' I asked. 'At 6 AM,' sir,' he replied. SIX AM!? Four hours in the dark, in the middle of nowhere? 'That won't do and besides,' I pleaded indignantly, 'Hari and Claudia [his bosses] told me the ferry was 24/7.' 'Yes sir,' he replied, 'but because there were no customers earlier in the night, the ferry captain has gone to bed.' 'Well, can't we wake him up?' I demanded, 'Where exactly is this captain?' 'On the other side of the river, sir, in Maharashtra,' he said.

My response: 'Okay, then start beeping your horn and flashing your lights.' The ludicrousness of my demands didn't occur to me until much later. But there we were, in the pitch-black dark of the night, in a forest on the edge of a massive river, honking and flashing headlights as if we were in a traffic jam in Manhattan. Lots of flashing and beeping. Nothing. More beeping, more flashing. Still nothing. Then, in the distance, I heard the distinctive splutter of a diesel engine starting up. A small, dark shadow was making its way across the water towards us. The closer it got, the more it struck me that 'ferry' was an overly generous description for the rivercraft. 'Raft' would have been more accurate. The entire contraption was only slightly wider than our car. Waking the captain suddenly didn't seem like such a great improvement on the situation.

This was a one-car ferry with two crewmen. One man's job was to tie the ropes; the other was there to keep the engine running. As an aid to navigation and a mechanism against being carried out to sea on the outgoing tide, the ferry ran along a cable suspended between the two shores. When it finally arrived, my driver dutifully parked on the very small mobile pontoon. With automobile in place, there was hardly any ferry left visible, but neither the captain (the one who had to keep the engine running) nor the crewman with the ropes seemed in the least bit worried. Off we went, into the darkness, bound for Maharashtra.

When we were roughly halfway, the cable – really just a big old grease-stained rope – broke, and we started to drift upstream with the incoming tide. It could have been worse: we could have been drifting out to sea with the outgoing tide. And then it did get worse. The engine stopped. Judging from the head-scratching and animated conversation between our two guides, this was not the first time the raft had broken free or conked out. We were really starting to pick up speed – in the wrong direction – and the raft, without the forward push of the engine, was significantly less stable. We were

drifting down a big river on a tiny raft and the two men in charge didn't seem to be doing much about it, except adding ever more greasy bits and pieces to the pile of engine parts that had started to accumulate on deck.

And then the most remarkable thing happened, the thing that makes India like no other place on the planet. Against all odds the captain managed to restart the engine. With a tooth-grinding crunch, he threw the old diesel into gear and slowly, ever so slowly, we started to make some headway. An eternity later, just when the first rays of daylight had started to appear, we finally docked on the other side of the river. I felt like Moses crossing the Red Sea. Meanwhile, my driver was winning the award for obliviousness bordering on insanity. He had been napping in the car throughout the entire pre-dawn drama and drove off the raft as if he had just made a left-hand turn at a traffic light.

Fort Tiracol, which was now visible in the golden light of dawn, was certainly a sight for sore eyes. Built by the colonial Portuguese three centuries ago on a strategic headland flanked by massive stretches of deserted sandy beaches, it's a beautiful example of the seafaring nation's talent for creating architecture that implies imperial strength, yet reflects the beauty of its tropical setting. Painted white and a rich shade of yellow, the fort is built on the water's edge, around a beautifully ornate church cradled within its protective walls. It's a handsome monument in a spectacular location, with the waves of the Indian Ocean lapping against its stone foundations. But

the outstanding feature is what the owners have done to it. Or not done to it, to be exact. Unlike many grand historic buildings in India that have been converted into hotels and then divided into box-like rooms, Tiracol has kept its original interior architecture. The spaces, especially the guest rooms, are vast, and most visitors get an entire apartment instead of just a room. Hari and Claudia have managed to preserve the fort without sacrificing comfort or convenience, and they have done this in their signature contemporary style. It's a sexy combination of colonial grandeur, exotic tropical surroundings and laid-back modern sophistication.

By the time the mid-morning sun was up, shining on the sandy beaches and azure water that define the beautiful headland, the ferry (mis)adventure seemed a distant memory.

JOSÉ IGNACIO

URUGUAY

LA POSADA DEL FARO

*Minimalist modernity among the endless
dunes and crashing surf of Uruguay's
rugged Atlantic coast*

A simple splash of colour on a wall announces that you're in South
America. The beaches and dunes may look like Martha's Vineyard but
the colour of this living room in La Posada del Faro tells you otherwise.

In a place with skies so blue they're almost purple in some lights,
La Posada del Faro's simple, white architectural elements – such as
whitewashed walls and bleached wicker – contrast beautifully
with the intensity of the backdrop.

La Posada del Faro is a modern whitewashed bunker nestled in the wild, windswept sand dunes of Uruguay's Atlantic coast. It doesn't look or feel like a hotel – it's more like an architect's beach house.

As the crow flies, the tiny village of José Ignacio is not far from Punta del Este but in terms of ambience and aesthetics they're as distant from each other as it is possible to be. Punta del Este sounded so wonderfully exotic that I had been looking forward to visiting it from the moment I started planning a trip to South America. Surely, on a continent famous for its thousands of exotic beach destinations, this would have to be one of the best, especially since it's so popular, judging purely from the number of flights that depart daily from Buenos Aires for Punta.

When I finally got there, it was such a letdown. Punta looks more or less like Cancún, but without the turquoise sea and the white beaches (Punta has big sandy beaches but they're not white). It's a mini Miami, a jumble of concrete apartment buildings, hotels and casinos; all touristy and developed, like the Gold Coast in Queensland. It was the polar opposite of exotic. Why would people come here, I wondered. (I later discovered that a lot of Brazilians come because of the casinos, and the residents of Buenos Aires come because they have no beaches of their own.)

Driving past all the high-rise developments and shopping arcades and marinas, I had almost given up on finding my dream: a simple place with character, on a deserted stretch of beach.

But Punta doesn't last long. As you start to drive north, the landscape quickly changes from high-rise hotel and apartment blocks to low-rise buildings to smaller clusters of wooden houses. Then, as the road continues alongside the ocean, the buildings stop altogether. All that remains are forests and patches of farmland on one side of the road and long stretches of big, sweeping sand dunes and views of crashing waves on the other.

It's beautiful, but it didn't look like South America to me – more like the west coast of France, or the beaches of Cape Cod or Montauk on the north Atlantic coast of the USA. It was odd to realize that certain places in the southern hemisphere can look so similar to places in the northern hemisphere. Squint and the only difference between the beaches of the Hamptons and Uruguay's Atlantic coast is the timing of the seasons.

Nevertheless, by the time I got to José Ignacio, I was smitten.

Nestled among the dunes, José Ignacio is nothing more than a handful of shacks on a stretch of unspoiled Atlantic beach that seems to go on forever. It's my kind of town. Everything is wooden and weather-beaten. Even the supermarket is in an elegantly distressed timber warehouse. I could easily understand why the author Martin Amis chose to live here for several years. It's hard to imagine a finer place for hunkering down to write a book.

José Ignacio is where the people from Buenos Aires and Montevideo who prefer the sophisticated simplicity of the beach to

the bling of Punta spend their summers. Hidden in the folds of the sand dunes, on a stretch of beach that looks like the set of a 1960s surf film, they hang out in what must be the most stylish and laid-back beach club in the world: a collection of timber-plank walkways that criss-cross the dunes. The walkways are furnished with big slouchy cushions and decorated with incredibly tanned and fit people who look like they never eat.

And yet they must, because José Ignacio has some of the most famous restaurants in South America. Unassuming and low-key, housed in faded timber shacks, they have given this tiny speck in the dunes a massive reputation for food.

La Posada del Faro is one of the few places in José Ignacio – apart from the lighthouse that dominates the bend in the coastline – that is not made of weather-beaten timber. It is a modernist bungalow, the kind of beach house that might be perfect for Tom Ford's next film, a collection of bold geometric angles and slab-shaped surfaces that contrast beautifully with the organic curves of the surrounding dunes. The rooms are like the exterior: pared-down and white, with big expanses of glass that give splendid views of the sea. But the thing that really sets it apart is the vibe: very relaxed in a simple but sophisticated way, which is exactly what you want from a house on the beach. Some guests bodysurf, run on the beach or build sand castles with their kids; others just read books or sleep. Everyone goes their own way. It's the ultimate chilled-out atmosphere.

La Posada del Faro is the kind of place where I could imagine settling in for weeks, which, not surprisingly, is exactly what many guests do every January. The problem, of course, is that there aren't enough of its sand dunes and salty air to go around, so there are plans underway for several new hotels in José Ignacio. Hopefully the new developments will be discreet and designed with sensitivity to the location, but I have my doubts.

In the meantime, chuffed with my new discovery, I boarded my flight back to Buenos Aires. 'You look like you've had a good time' said the lady next to me in seat 7G. 'Yes,' I beamed back, 'I love it when I find a place in an amazing location that's authentic and unspoiled and affordable. Who wouldn't?'

'Which place is that?' she asked, nodding knowingly when I responded 'José Ignacio'. 'Where else have you been?' she asked. 'Oh,' I answered, 'all over South America.' She looked quite dubious. 'Really?' she said, 'Like where?' So I took a deep breath and rattled off my most recent itinerary: 'Buenos Aires to Bariloche, Bariloche to El Calafate in Patagonia. Then on to the Perito Moreno glacier. Back to Buenos Aires, over to Iguazú then three hours in the back of a truck through the jungle and eventually by canoe to a remote *centro biologico* on the Iguazú River. Back to Buenos Aires, over to Santiago, Chile, and then a flight to the Atacama Desert. Back to Santiago, over to Lima, then to Cuzco and then by train to Machu Picchu, back to Lima, over to São Paulo, up to Porto Seguro, down

The wildness of the windswept, sunbaked sand dunes on the rugged coastline outside contrasts with the serenity of the pared-down, whitewashed interior, which is occasionally enlivened by splashes of colour from local artworks or the odd feature wall. It's a simple but powerful formula that makes the appeal of La Posada del Faro timeless and enduring. This is one place that will not change – it doesn't need to.

to Trancoso, then by boat to Corumbau, back to São Paulo, down to Picinguaba. Back to São Paulo, down to Punta and then to José Ignacio…' I stopped for breath. I thought she would be asleep by now but she was looking at me intently and then, after a very effective pause, she said, 'So you haven't been to Venezuela?' The stunned look on my face was all the answer she needed. 'And you haven't been to Bolivia? Or Ecuador? Or Colombia?' Taking my continued silence as a yes, she continued, victoriously, 'So, you haven't really been all over South America. Have you?'

Game, set, and match to the passenger in 7G from…Venezuela.

That's what you get for showing off. She was right, of course. I hadn't been all over South America. Not by a long shot. No matter how much you travel, there is always somewhere you haven't been.

PORT-CROS
FRANCE

LE MANOIR

*The only establishment on an untamed
and little-known island just off the
swanky Côte d'Azur*

There is one place in the south of France that is untouched by the suburban blight that has spoiled much of the Riviera. Just off the coast of Hyères, away from the endless developments of boxy imitation farmhouses built for English, Dutch and Scandinavian tourists eager for a place in the sun, sits the enigmatic, pristine island of Port-Cros. Port-Cros is the least well-known of the Îles d'Hyères, a trio of islands (Porquerolles and Le Levant are its better-known sisters) that featured in the writing of F. Scott Fitzgerald and Jean Cocteau, for whom these tiny dots in the French Mediterranean encapsulated the irresistible, languid sensuousness of the Midi without the decadent and nouveau-riche atmosphere of nearby Cannes, Nice and Monte Carlo.

Port-Cros does not have shopping centres, high-rise hotels or six-lane highways. In fact, it has no roads at all. It is a haven for anyone nostalgic for a time when this part of France inspired artists, poets and writers with its idyllic beauty and tranquil lifestyle.

Here the Mediterranean looks as it ought to: clear and pristine, with multiple layers of underwater growth that give the sea a vivid emerald-green hue. The land, too, is wild and unspoiled, with old-growth forest covering the the island's rocky, hilly landscape. There are no holiday homes, hotels or campgrounds on Port-Cros, just the odd defensive fort built by Napoleon two hundred years ago, and an elegant former hunting lodge of similar vintage, which now serves as the island's only hotel: the very charming Le Manoir.

This building is in fact the very reason that Port-Cros managed to avoid the fate of the rest of the south of France. Port-Cros was originally a private island belonging to the family who built the hunting lodge. When the last direct descendant died he bequeathed the entire island to the nation, with a very strict and specific deed of gift. His family's beloved Port-Cros was not to be turned into yet another *plage* (beach) of the Côte d'Azur. It would have only one hotel – the former hunting lodge – and the concession to manage it would remain with a member of the family. The rest of the island would be left 'wild' and the government would be obliged to pledge resources to maintain it as such: a team of marine biologists and scientists from the Department of Forestry would be engaged full-time to monitor the unique ecological experiment of returning the island to its natural state.

That's not to say the island is off-limits to visitors. There are ferries every day in the summer to Port-Cros's tiny harbour from Le Lavandou on the mainland. Visitors can enjoy extraordinary hikes, with views of some of the most pristine bays and beaches in the entire Mediterranean, along steep rocky cliffs that require goat-like nimbleness to navigate. Passengers are counted out when they disembark and counted back in before the last ferry leaves in the afternoon. The only way you can stay overnight on the island is as a guest at Le Manoir, discreetly hidden among the casuarina trees and weeping willows that surround the island's only bay.

The experience of staying at Le Manoir is as authentic as the island itself. It feels as if you've landed in an Yves Montand film from the early 1950s. Decorated in a casual, shabby-chic version of Provence style with wicker chairs, white linen, floral curtains, black-and-white tiled floors, wrought-iron tables and wooden shutters to cope with the afternoon heat, the hotel seduces with its character and charm. The luxuries it offers are those of simplicity, natural beauty and privacy – rare commodities, especially in the south of France. Le Manoir has that dark quiet that the south used to have. It's dusty and old-fashioned in the most refined sense. You half expect to find Hemingway writing in one of the wicker chairs under the weeping willows with a Pernod and ice and a carafe of water on the table beside him. The heat, the constant clicking of the cicadas, the sunflowers in the nearby fields, the sailboats at anchor in the bay and even the Mini Moke that the hotel uses to pick up its guests at the jetty all give this place a magic that has nothing to do with money and everything to do with authenticity and romance.

There is nothing deliberately stylish about Le Manoir, yet it is one of the most stylish places I know. Dinner is a great example. In the south of France people eat late – great for adults, but not so great for children who need to go to bed. So the dining room – the one with the black-and-white tiled floor and the 1950s wrought-iron furniture and floral curtains – serves a separate dinner at 7 PM for for the younger guests dressed in their pyjamas. The parents are served an aperitif while the kids eat. Later, after the little ones are tucked in, guests wander to a spot next to the harbour where tables set with white linen and silver stand in the dusty terracotta-coloured dirt under a pergola covered with vines, looking out over the water. Because it's an island and the only other guests are those fortunate enough to stay at Le Manoir, you can enjoy your meal without worrying about your child's safety – yet another way that the hotel transports you to a world without care.

A world without care, perhaps, but still with plenty of adventure to offer adults and children alike. We forget how wonderful wild is. No umbrellas, no reclining loungers, no signs, no crowds, no music, no traffic, no shops and almost no buildings. Stripped of all these things, your focus returns to nature. You realize that you don't need anything, not even a towel, to go for a swim, and that that warm sand feels more sensuous on your feet than plastic shoes; you discover that seeing fish underwater in their natural habitat is much more rewarding than visiting the aquarium. Port-Cros's beaches seem even more beautiful because they are hidden and you have to hike steep and rugged trails to get to them.

All this, I think, is what the last surviving heir of the family who once owned this extraordinary island wanted to leave behind: a chance to experience the romantic beauty of the south of France before it vanished completely. Thanks to his generosity, Port-Cros now stands as a thriving example of how things used to be – and, more importantly, how they ought to be.

Apart from the splendid isolation offered by what is essentially a private lodge
on a private island, the most captivating feature of idyllic Port-Cros is the
magnificent manner in which the island has been returned to its natural state.
A dedicated team of marine biologists working year-round have managed
to get the beaches, the sea bed and even the underwater vegetation back
to how they would have been hundreds of years ago.

Tucked away under a verdant canopy of casuarina and eucalyptus trees, Le Manoir is situated
on the edge of a picturesque natural harbour. Discreet, charming and bewitchingly timeless,
it's the south of France we all fantasize about.

PALM SPRINGS
USA
KORAKIA PENSIONE

*Moroccan architecture and bohemian style in
the shadow of the ochre-coloured mountains
of Palm Springs, California*

It was the last stop on my Route 1 road trip from San Francisco to Los Angeles, which took me south along the Pacific coast and then east, inland to Palm Springs, the desert retreat on the edge of the Mojave made legendary by the Rat Pack and the stars of Hollywood's golden age.

My son Louis, who had just turned one, joined me on the drive, along with his bed, special mattress, pram, car seat, full menagerie of stuffed animals, extensive library of books and a travel refrigerator filled with infant yoghurts. The only car that all of his stuff would fit into was the largest SUV commercially available. It came in only one livery: black with tinted windows, which made me looked like a drug smuggler from Medellín.

The beginning and end of the day, when I had to load or unload the 'black beast', were not my favourite parts of the trip. I felt like an itinerant labourer for an indecisive circus: 'Put up the tent here! No, I've changed my mind – we're moving on! Take it down and put it back into the truck.' During most of the trip we never spent more than one night in one place, with the exception of the Post Ranch Inn in Big Sur, where the treehouse we were lodged in was spectacular…and spectacularly scary, offering no less than twenty-eight different ways (I counted!) for a one-year-old to commit hara-kiri.

After five days as my son's personal roadie, I was looking forward to getting to Palm Springs and staying put for a while. In Los Angeles, a friend whose taste and sense of style I usually trust suggested that I check out this quirky place in Palm Springs called Korakia Pensione. 'It's like being in Morocco,' she said by way of enticement. 'OK,' I said, 'I will try to find it.' In fact I had no intention of going to a 'Moroccan' place – I've never liked themed hotels and I've been to Morocco often enough to know that I prefer the real thing. Oblivious to my reluctance, my friend promised that Korakia was easy to find – the last place set against the mountains after you leave the main drag. Easy or not, there was no way we were going there. It all sounded a bit too Vegas for me.

By the time I arrived in Palm Springs I had forgotten all about my friend's suggestion. I was busy photographing and writing about motels like Orbit In that do a convincing job of recreating the Sinatra era with retro design, kidney-shaped swimming pools and slightly cheesy cocktail bars. Then, completely by accident, I stumbled upon Korakia while I was walking around the neighbourhood. As I wandered into the street closest to the mountains, the prettiest and most isolated street in town, I saw the unmistakable arches of a house so convincingly Moroccan that it could have been transported brick by brick from Tangier. Not only was the architecture convincing in every detail but it actually looked right for its surroundings – and much more so than the faux haciendas and 1960s modernist bungalows that make up much of Palm Springs. Set against the backdrop of the barren but beautiful San Jacinto mountains the 'Moroccan place' looked completely at home. Although Korakia is still within walking distance of the bars and restaurants of the main street, it is isolated enough that the fantasy world it inhabits is not spoiled by the clashing aesthetics of its neighbours.

The decor and architecture are inspiring and seductive on their own, but the most endearing quality of Korakia is its ambience. If I was an artist I would come here to paint. The rooms are like lofts and there are plenty of hidden spaces – private courtyards, personal swimming pools and small gardens stashed all over the property – that cater to the urge for creative inspiration and the desire for privacy without the feeling of being cooped up.

Korakia was built by a Scottish artist named Gordon Coutts in 1924, when Palm Springs was little more than empty desert. The Rat Pack and the Hollywood crowd had not yet arrived; Frank Sinatra was an apple-cheeked baby in Hoboken, New Jersey; and the Canadian 'snowbirds' were still just that: birds (today, of course, they are Canadians who arrive in mid-winter for a desperately needed fix of UV rays.)

Dar Maroc, as the villa was originally called, recalled the time when Coutts had lived in Tangier, during the era when the Moroccan town was first becoming a bohemian hotspot, attracting artists, writers, spies, mercenaries and deposed aristocrats. The heady atmosphere must have made a lasting impression on the young Coutts, who, when he eventually settled in America, not only sought a place with a similar climate but also built – entirely from memory – a house that would remind him of the magic of Morocco. At the time, Palm Springs was a small artists' colony and Coutts's domed Moroccan folly, with its whitewashed battlements and huge wooden doors, became its cultural centre, where the flamboyant flame-haired artist would tell tales of his exotic travels against the spectacular backdrop of the mountains to guests who eventually included Rudolph Valentino and Errol Flynn, to name but a few. Even Winston Churchill is rumoured to have painted in the studio that is now one of Korakia's guest rooms.

In the winter, when most of America is dealing with shovels, galoshes, hats, scarves and coats, you can wake here in the crystal-clear desert air under a cloudless steel-blue sky and savour your first coffee on a terrace surrounded by cacti and palm trees, admiring the copper-coloured boulders of the mountains as they are warmed by the golden rays of the early morning sun. For me, this is what Palm Springs is all about: not the many boutiques, restaurants and bars that are feverishly reviewed by countless magazines and websites; not the golf courses that threaten to empty the surrounding water reservoirs; and not even the famous modernist bungalows that the fashion world has fallen in love with.

Korakia, with its unique history, highly individual environment and special sense of isolation, returns you to the true essence of Palm Springs: the simple magnificence of the Mojave desert and the mountains of southern California.

What I love most about Korakia Pensione is its bohemian flair. It feels like a
place made by artists for artists. There's no wow or bling; instead, Korakia
seduces you with its mellow sophistication, which comes out in details
such as massive slabs of flagstone in a bathroom or an artful still life of
flea market finds in a guest room. Korakia does not try to impress, but
I still find it one of the most impressive places in the USA.

NUSA LEMBONGAN
BALI
WAKA NUSA

A big volcano, fresh fish, good surf and
faultless simplicity on a tiny island
off the coast of Bali

Unless you're a surfer you've probably never heard of this island.

Nusa Lembongan is a tiny speck off the southern coast of Bali, with beautiful beaches, crystal-clear water and an unbeatable panoramic view of Bali's largest and most imposing mountain, Mount Agung. The island probably would have remained completely unknown were it not for a bunch of Australian hippies who arrived in Bali in the early 1970s. They settled in thatched *losmens* at a beach called Kuta, which became a regular destination for 'soul surfers' who wanted to 'drop out' in exotic Bali. In Bali's unique version of Hinduism, the most feared monsters live in the sea, so the locals regarded surfing as a extraordinarily heroic pursuit and welcomed the arriving long-haired counter-culture characters with interest.

Soon Sanur, a blossoming tourist village just down the coast from Kuta, was also attracting a small group of surfers. In August 1971, its visitors included Albert Falzon, an Australian surfer and filmmaker who had come to Bali to finish his surf film *Morning of the Earth*. In search of the ultimate surfing experience, Falzon and his crew headed further down the coast to where swirls of white water had been seen spewing into the air. Off the cliffs of the Bukit Peninsula, near a temple named Uluwatu, they found a heart-stopping panorama of perfect waves, cleaner, bigger, and more consistent than any in Hawaii, the birthplace of surfing. Uluwatu became legendary, and for a time was considered the best surfing location in the world.

Then the surfers started to do the maths: if this one corner of Indonesia had such amazing waves, surely there were hundreds of other breaks waiting to be discovered. Another surfer, an intrepid 'trust-fund traveller' from southern California named Bob Laverty, noticed a wave-line from a plane as he passed over the south-western tip of Java and organized an expedition to an area called Grajagan to check it out. 'G-Land', as it is known today, entered the list of legendary surf spots with its mile-long double-overhead barrels. 'G-Land' was followed by 'Padang-Padang', 'One Palm', 'Scar Reef' and 'Desert Point', among others. Indonesia's seemingly endless supply of undiscovered surfing spots fuelled the quest of all adventure-loving surfers to find a spot where they wouldn't have to share the line-up. That's how they found Nusa Lembongan. But you don't have to be a surfer to appreciate this place.

Nusa Lembongan is unspoiled and natural, the way Bali used to be. There are few roads and no shopping centres, restaurants or surf shops. The local population of several thousand people is divided between just two villages and most still rely on farming and fishing for a living. Waka Nusa, one of the local resorts, has stayed in touch with this blissfully simple way of life. A small compound of ten thatched villas on the beach of Tanjung Sanghiang Bay, Waka Nusa has no air-conditioning, television, Wi-Fi or telephones. A larger thatched structure with a sand floor serves as the restaurant where guests meet for dinner and the menu on offer is always 'the catch of the day'.

The most spectacular time on Nusa Lembongan is early morning, when the active volcano Agung, Bali's 'mother mountain', shows its profile through the blue-grey mist. To sit at the edge of the beach, in the dull warmth of early morning sun, with your toes in the sand, having your first coffee and contemplating breakfast while you gaze at Bali's imposing mountains, is so special that it's spiritual, whether you believe in God or not. It doesn't surprise me that devout (and Harley-riding) Balinese Hindus Ketut Siandana and his brothers, who also built Waka di Ume (see page 191), decided to found a resort here.

Waka Nusa has a big seafaring catamaran called Wakalouka and guests get transported from Bali to Nusa Lembongan by sail, the slowest and most adventurous way to go. When I made the journey the boat left just before lunch. The first part involved a bit of motoring, past some of the huge hotels that have sprung up on Bali's beaches, but once the catamaran reached the Badung Strait, the channel that divides Bali and Nusa Lembongan, the sails went up and we started surging ahead at speed. A group of dolphins joined us and swam in formation right in front of the boat, making occasional flights across the bow to show off, with the odd mid-air flip for good measure.

We then sailed for a while next to an enormous blue-black sperm whale. The guests were ecstatic at this close encounter but I had read enough tales of maritime mishaps to know that an overly enthusiastic whale can easily sink a yacht with just one powerful head-butt or swipe of its tail. Our huge friend hung around for a while, easily keeping pace with the catamaran even though we were really flying in the stiff winds off the coast. Eventually he gave a loud, scary snort, threw up a plume of water and disappeared under the surface. It was an incredible experience to see such a majestic creature up close, but I have to admit I was relieved when it was over.

In the late afternoon we arrived on the sandy crescent that is home to Waka Nusa. Although pure simplicity is the order of the day, this tiny compound is nonetheless quite innovative from a design perspective. The main public area is a large, open structure with a thatched roof, inspired by the Indonesian longhouse, the traditional tribal dwelling that is still in use in Borneo and on the more remote islands. In essence, it is simply a roof that provides shelter from the rain and the sun. And that's all you need in a place like this. Guest accommodation is designed with the same utilitarian simplicity. Each guest gets their own bungalow set back from the beach. Although the bungalows appear compact from the outside, they are deceptively spacious, owing to their round design. Each has a big bed in the middle, surrounded by a cosy living area with a built-in banquette that follows the curve of the hut; the wall behind the bed conceals a bathroom that also follows the curve of the house. There is also a small spa right on the beach that is perfect for doing exactly what those Australian hippies set out to do in the early 1970s: drop out, kick back and tune in.

Waka Nusa is for the 'soul surfer' in us all.

Built no more than a stone's throw from the beach, Waka Nusa's unique guest
bungalows combine a round architectural form with a cone-shaped thatched
roof, offering a complex blend of tradition, modernity and clever use of space.
With polished concrete floors, splendid four-poster canopy beds, cosy living
areas and unusual curved bathrooms, they are innovative gems worthy of
their idyllic location.

ARIZONA
USA
RANCHO DE IA OSA

*Cowboys, colour and cacti on a ranch in
the dusty heart of Apache country*

Rancho De La Osa is the kind of place you would see in an old Western like *The Magnificent Seven*, with tough guys like Yul Brynner riding black horses across a dusty landscape punctuated by tall cacti.

The ranch is a ruggedly attractive 'spread', as they call it in Arizona, in what was once Apache territory, not far from the legendary Rio Grande. The surroundings are beautiful in a scorched and unforgiving sort of way: a pale blue horizon defined by distant craggy peaks that flatten out on top, with the odd rocky stream snaking its way across the terrain. It's a perfect landscape for exploring on horseback. During the day you ride out to help herd cattle for the ranch and at night you stay in one of the cabins adjoining an adobe hacienda that looks like it could have been decorated by Frida Kahlo, with vivid indigo-blue walls painted with red, orange and green geometric designs and hung with Native American handcrafts, including Navajo rugs and blankets. The effect is at once seductive and authentically Southwestern. Mexico is not far away and the influence of what was once New Spain is visible throughout the hacienda, from the solid oak furniture and wrought-iron chandeliers to the old mission bell that still hangs outside a building that was once the trading post (now the bar) and is rung to announce dinner.

I honestly don't remember how I found out about this place but I will definitely never forget the journey I took to get there.

I had been driving around the American Southwest working on a *HIP Hotels* book and found myself in a part of Texas called the Big Bend. If you ever want to grasp just how big Texas is, try driving from the Big Bend to anywhere else in the United States – it's at least twelve hours before you even leave the state. I started the day by putting foot to pedal and ploughing a straight line several hundred miles north-west from the Big Bend to Bisbee, Arizona, where there is a hotel made up entirely of vintage Airstream caravans. Each guest gets to stay in their own silver-clad, bullet-shaped American icon. How cool is that? When I finally got to Bisbee the Airstreams were indeed magnificent, but nobody had told me that they offered panoramic views of…an abandoned mine. I had planned to spend the night there but instead decided to push on to Rancho De La Osa. On the map the ranch is between Tucson, Arizona, and Nogales, Mexico, near a town called Rio Rico. According to the driving instructions I was first to drive north-west to Tucson on I-10 and then head south towards Nogales on I-40. It was definitely the long way round. The other option was to take a smaller road that went straight west through a town called Sonoita, then south-west on a road that ended at Rio Rico. On the map both roads were depicted by broken black lines. I didn't know what this meant and I didn't care. I just wanted to get to Rancho De La Osa as fast as possible.

I soon discovered that 'broken black line' meant 'not paved'. A four-wheel-drive would have been fine but I was in a completely

unsuitable standard-issue rental car – white, no less. It was late; I had already been driving for hours and I just wanted to get there, so I convinced myself that my rental car would make it. How bad could the road really be? The question was answered by the extremely loud and disturbing banging noise that my poor little white sedan began to make as its undercarriage was pounded into the uneven dirt road. Distracted by the never-ending succession of protruding boulders and gaping potholes, it did not occur to me that I had not seen another vehicle for the better part of two hours, until a four-wheel-drive Bronco marked 'US Border Patrol' pulled into view.

They pulled me over.

An officer, wearing exactly the kind of reflective sunglasses that you would expect the US Border Patrol to wear, approached my car in a slow, measured way. 'Sir, do you know why we pulled you over?' he asked.

'No?' was my feeble response, with question mark audible.

'Sir', he continued, leaning on the window seal, 'there are only two kinds of vehicles that use this road: vehicles smuggling illegal immigrants and vehicles smuggling illegal drugs. Which are you?'

'Um, neither', I replied, in what I very much hoped was the tone of someone not worth arresting. 'I'm a travel writer and photographer and I'm on my way to visit a place called Rancho De La Osa, just outside Rio Rico,' pleading as if I had done something very wrong and very stupid (which was at least half-right).

It was apparently the most amusing thing that these officers had seen all week: a tourist with an unpronounce-able last name, all by himself in his NON-four-wheel-drive rental car, on one of the most dangerous roads in the USA.

'Well, Sir,' said my new friend, clearly trying not to laugh, 'if you come across another car and it's not us, you better start praying, because these smug-glers are a jittery, nervous bunch and they might mistake your Ford for an unmarked car, if you get my drift.'

I got it. (Subtlety was not their strong suit.) They also helpfully let me know that it would be dark in less than two hours and there was no way that I would be in Rio Rico by then.

I felt like I was in one of those creepy David Lynch-style films that are always set in a godforsaken place in the middle of nowhere where nothing happens for ages, but you know that when something finally does it will be horribly and unimaginably brutal. But I was as far from Bisbee as I was from Rio Rico, and it was same road, same risk in both directions, so I figured I might as well just keep going. I drove that poor little Ford like it was a turbo-charged Range Rover. It hammered the bejesus out of the undercarriage and I didn't care, just cranked up the music to drown out the scraping and banging as I ploughed towards Rio Rico like a trucker on stimulants.

Just before 8 PM that night, after four hours on the road from hell, I pulled triumphantly – and gratefully – up to the front gate of Rancho De La Osa. My hosts must have thought I was a bit strange because

If you're a fan of legendary westerns such as *The Magnificent Seven*, Rancho De La Osa will look familiar. But make no mistake: this is not a Hollywood 'dude ranch'. The landscape is real and so are the chores. If you choose to ride a horse after breakfast, for instance, you will be expected to chip in with rounding up the cattle or herding them to new pastures. It's hot and dusty work but the scenery is magnificent and the experience is something you will never forget.

I was overly complimentary to everyone, even by American standards, and probably had a crazed euphoric look on my face. How could
they know I had just lived through my own version of *No Country for
Old Men*?

Oh, and the poor car? Not a word from the staff at the rental agency
when I returned it. They obviously never check the undercarriage.

After a long day in the saddle, there's something very special about relaxing on one of Rancho De La Osa's verandas. Sitting in an Adirondack chair painted in hot desert colours, surrounded by monumental cacti, you'll find the veranda the perfect place to enjoy a cold Corona as the scorching heat of the Arizona sun starts to abate.

AEOLIAN ISLANDS
ITALY
HOTEL RAYA

*Minimalist volcanic chic in the
remote Aeolian Islands*

Inspired by the whitewashed simplicity of the Greek islands, Hotel Raya, on the island of Panarea, is a refined minimalist vision sitting on a rugged outcrop of volcanic stone in the azure waters of the Tyrrhenian Sea.

All you need to wear in the Aeolian Islands is a sarong, a T-shirt, a bathing suit and some sunglasses to cope with the blinding whiteness of it all.

My first visit to Panarea was short. Very short. I was on my way to Australia for a family funeral, and Panarea was one of the stops the ship – which is the only way to get from the Aeolian Islands to the mainland off-season – made en route from Sicily to Naples.

Even though I was only on the island for a few hours, it was long enough to notice that a few things about Panarea looked odd. Where were the cars? The buses? The trucks? And the mopeds? An Italian seaside town without a pack of teenagers aimlessly racing through the streets on their souped-up 'sewing machines' seemed peculiar; in fact, there were not even any bicycles to be seen. The architecture seemed so pristine, attractive and uniform: all the buildings were the same shape, the same colour and almost the same height. The effect was fascinatingly tasteful, a perfect contrast to the rugged beauty of the natural surroundings – as if Dolce & Gabbana had teamed up with James Cameron of *Avatar* fame to create a 'virtual' Italian island.

I resolved to come back to explore this unexpected gem in the summer, when the hydrofoils and SeaCats departing from Naples can whizz you to Panarea in less than four hours. In the meantime I did some homework.

Not too long ago the Aeolian Islands weren't so idyllic. They were some of the poorest communities in Italy, especially Panarea, the smallest of the islands, which had the least going for it. It was flat, rocky and barren. Fishing was about the only way to make a living, but the Italian mainland was too far away to be viable as a market, so the locals could only sell their fish to each other and a few close neighbours. No wonder most of the islanders eventually emigrated to Australia. Today, if you listen carefully, you will occasionally hear the odd English word pronounced with a distinctive Aussie twang in the middle of a conversation in Italian. The speakers are the grandsons and granddaughters of immigrants who have come back to see the 'old country' where their ancestors were born.

It's difficult to imagine how abandoned, barren, remote Panarea aquired the uber-chic status it has today. The story centres around a globetrotting couple, Paolo Tilche and Myriam Beltrami, who arrived here in the 1960s. By then most of the population had emigrated and just a handful of families continued the age-old struggle to make a living from the sea. But Myriam and Paolo didn't see a hapless piece of sea-bound volcanic rock – they saw a place of exquisite, untouched beauty, blessed with the clearest emerald-green water in the Mediterranean. Panarea was exactly what they were looking for. Here they could realize the lifestyle they had fantasized about: swimming, diving and fishing. Panarea offered a return to nature without the high prices and trashy tourism of other better-known islands in the Mediterranean. They built a house on a small rocky outcrop with a view of Stromboli and soon their friends were lining up to share the newfound island paradise. In those days there was, at best, a boat once every two weeks that stopped at Panarea but this did not deter the island's new fans, so intoxicated were they by its uncomplicated beauty and charm. Myriam and Paolo's house, constantly expanding to accomodate the steady stream of guests, eventually became a hotel (today's Hotel Raya).

When their friends started to ask the couple to find them pieces of land on which to build their own houses, Miriam and Paolo became the de facto gatekeepers of the island's new aesthetic. This is why the architecture on Panarea is so uniform. Drawing on skills learned during his stint on the Greek island of Hydra, Paolo designed everything according to a master plan, inspired by the buildings he had seen there.

Like Panarea, Hydra is small and quite spartan but very popular with designers and architects who commute by ferry from Athens, because it is so unspoiled and charming. It didn't get that way by accident, however, but as a result of careful and strict planning. Cars, buses, trucks, motorbikes and even bicycles are not allowed, so there is no need for paved roads; tiny pathways and trails suffice. Residents are obliged to follow a very strict building code that prescribes traditional designs and colour schemes and strictly prohibits any buildings over two storeys high. The result? A high quality of life, blissfully free of noise and pollution, including visual pollution.

Like Hydra, the building code on Panarea is absolute. All properties are designed in the traditional Aeolian manner and conform to a strict decorative scheme, with whitewashed walls accented with contrasting details painted powder blue, ochre yellow and terracotta pink. Even if you have no knowledge of Aeolian traditions, it simply looks and feels right. The effect, as you walk the winding paths that connect the houses to the island's beaches, is both visually stunning and quietly charming.

I did manage to make my way back to Panarea later that same summer. The first thing that struck me as I looked out from the terraces of Hotel Raya was the panoramic vista of the spitting, rumbling, smoke-spewing active volcano of Stromboli, another of the Aeolian islands. Hotel Raya was designed to face this spectacle, with terraces built on rocky outcrops into the sea known as the *pied dans l'eau* ('feet in the water'), where you can admire the volcano at breakfast, lunch and dinner. The entire hotel functions as an amphitheatre dedicated to this view, which is especially captivating at night, when the volcano glows as it spews steam and smoke.

The hotel has been cleverly divided into two parts. The building on the water, with its tables and terraces, is the central social hub, where all the eating, drinking and dancing is done. The guest rooms,

small whitewashed bungalows decorated with exotic ethnic pieces from Bali, are nestled into the surrounding hills, a 5-minute walk from the main building.

The logic behind this division is simple. Those who want to party can do so with abandon, and those who want to sleep can head up the hill, secure in the knowledge that they will not be disturbed by the noise.

With its seductive and rugged natural beauty and its stylishly sympathetic architectural style, Panarea is the ugly duckling of the Aeolian Islands that grew up to become a white (washed) swan

You can almost hear the conversations back in Australia: 'Gramps …what were you thinking? How could you leave a place as beautiful as that island? Couldn't you have at least kept a few acres?'

Three things make Panarea unlike any other place on the planet. The view
is volcanic, with the peak of Stromboli in the distance and black volcanic
outcrops in the sea nearby. The colours are almost exclusively white and
blue, with whitewashed houses contrasting with the vivid blue sky and
water. Finally, the architecture is disciplined in the extreme: every
building is the same height, style and colour.

There's no secret to the pristine whiteness of
Hotel Raya, just a lot of work. Each year,
without fail, the entire place gets a fresh
coat of white paint from top to bottom,
inside and out.

KERALA
INDIA

LAGOONA DAVINA

*Dugout canoes, thatched huts and elaborate
umbrellas in a picturesque lagoon
on Kerala's unspoiled coast*

Worry somewhere wonderful.

If ever such a phrase applied to a real place, it would be to this hidden retreat in a private lagoon on the unspoiled coast of Kerala.

It could even be the title of owner Davina's own story. Recently divorced, with grown children, and bored with her life as an estate agent in Britain, she decided it was time for a change. She sold her business and travelled to India, where she fell for the bewitching beauty and gentle nurturing lifestyle of Kerala. She decided that she wanted to create a splendid refuge for other women like her, a place where they could practise yoga, meditate, sit in the sun, walk on the beach or just do nothing at all, without the usual perils that accompany women travelling on their own.

It helped that she found the perfect spot. Davina's lagoon is what you imagine when you think of the perfect piece of Paradise: lush palm trees hanging over still, silvery water, flanked by massive stretches of golden sand that extend past old wooden fishing boats and nets drying in the sun to the mesmerizing blue of the Indian Ocean beyond – all in a place where it's usually warm and sunny and even when it rains, it's warm rain.

Despite the perfect weather, this is not a tourist destination. There are no nearby hotels, or restaurants, shops or bars, only the lagoon and the local fishermen on the beach, who do what they've done for hundreds of years: cast their nets and fish.

This suits Davina's customers perfectly. They haven't come for a holiday. They've come to put their ordinary lives on hold. They've come to learn about the extraordinary healing qualities of Ayurvedic massage, to go further in yoga than 'downward dog', and to eat freshly caught fish and newly picked mangoes. They are happy to live without air conditioning, television, mobile telephones and internet access, and to forget about traffic and commuting. They have come to concentrate, for once in their lives, on themselves and only on themselves.

Davina created exactly what she had in mind: an unashamedly 'me' kind of place. And it isn't only single women who have read *Eat Pray Love* who are drawn here. Men love it too. And why not? How wonderfully liberating to be able to indulge in yoga, massage and healthy food without your football mates making you feel silly about it. A week at Lagoona Davina will make a man more metrosexual than David Beckham.

Spending time here could change your life entirely. I know one person, a highly regarded professional in the travel industry, working for one of the world's fastest-growing airlines, who had dreamed of visiting Lagoona Davina. He could have gone anywhere, but he chose this place: the thatched bungalows on the edge of the lagoon with their eclectic bohemian interiors and the simple tables and handmade rattan chairs set outside in the shade of the overhanging palm trees where all the meals are served. He spent a few weeks at Lagoona Davina and never stopped talking about. It had obviously

pressed a few buttons in his psyche because not long after returning home he decided to redesign his entire life. He left his wife and moved to Berlin, where he got involved in the art world, learned German and met a beautiful German woman who became his girlfriend.

It's not the kind of radical transformation Lagoona Davina necessarily encourages, but then it doesn't disapprove either. It's a place that doesn't judge; where the many different paths to happiness are celebrated, an attitude that is profoundly embedded in the culture of India.

Years ago, on my first trip Kerala, I was taken to one of the few remaining timber palaces in southern India. The government guide was very knowledgable and he was keen to point out the prize feature of the palace: the mural room dedicated to Krishna. Here in the rather dark interior was a series of brightly coloured murals depicting the life of Krishna. It started with Krishna as a fat blue baby stealing *ghee* (butter) balls from the kitchen. The next mural had a blue teenage Krishna in a tree overhanging a river, laughing at an angry group of naked women who were unable to come out of the water because he had stolen their saris. The last mural depicted a mature blue Krishna, in the prime of his life, surrounded by scantily clad women and gorging himself on carnal pleasures. I told the guide that it seemed odd, at least to a Westerner like myself, that one of the most revered deities in India would be depicted as a naughty child, a delinquent teenager and a promiscuous grown man. My Indian

guide looked surprised, and, after a pause, replied, 'But surely…this is the life of a god!'

And that's what you get at Lagoona Davina – the life of a god: beautiful serene surroundings, warm tropical climate, fresh, health-giving food, and the daily indulgence of yoga sessions and therapeutic oil massages. The only problem is that no one will believe you when – or should I say if – you come back to your normal life.

When Marco Polo first started telling the stories of all his travels and adventures in the Far East, he was ridiculed and derided as 'Marco Millione' – the man of a million lies. It all seemed just too fanciful and dream-like to be true. Similarly, it's hard to believe that the Lagoona Davina lifestyle is so captivatingly exotic, yet so attainable. It makes you wonder what we are doing spending all our time in these cold climates, wearing shoes, going to offices and suffering on public transport.

Even the way you arrive at Lagoona Davina is like something straight out of an oriental myth. A car picks you up at Thiruvananthapuram Airport (which has to be the world's longest name for an airport!), and after a very short ride it stops beside a bridge. Your suitcases stay in the car but you are transferred to an exotic dugout canoe to continue your voyage to Lagoona Davina via the exquisite waterways that have made Kerala so legendary. The life of a god? Indeed – and all for the same price (per day) as a couple of tickets to the theatre.

Surely this is what we all dream about as
we trudge to work in the cold, pouring rain:
a palm-fringed lagoon overlooking a beach
festooned with wooden fishing boats in the
balmy tropics of India's southernmost state. This
was certainly Davina's dream and when she
found this lagoon, she made it her reality.

ÎLE DE RÉ
FRANCE
LE SÉNÉCHAL

*Chilled contemporary spaces cleverly disguised
behind a historic façade in the centre of
a quintessential French fishing town*

In August you won't find any Parisians in Paris.

You would be wrong to think that this is because they've all gone to the south of France. The Côte d'Azur is not considered French enough anymore. It's bad enough that Paris is invaded year-round by *les étrangers*; God forbid it should happen to their favourite beaches as well. The annual Parisian exodus to *les plages* is therefore kept as low profile as possible. Most people haven't heard of Île de Ré (yet) and the Parisians, who make up over 90 per cent of the island's population, are keen to keep it that way.

Île de Ré is an island of farms and fishing villages. It has no high-rise developments, timeshare apartments or suburban shopping centres. The strict protection of its villages, which include Saint-Martin-de-Ré, Les-Portes-en-Ré, Loix and Ars-en-Ré, and of its agrarian land means you will not find the over-building and tourist sprawl that has turned the south of France into a never-ending suburb. Instead you will find old stone walls, ancient town squares and untouched dunes.

The style of this small, flat island, just off the west coast of France, is rugged and nautical without being too cute or clichéd. But when it comes to shops and food it's clear there's a limit to how much Parisians are prepared to rough it. Small fromageries, boulangeries, poissoneries and charcuteries offering food of a quality equivalent to that available in the fancier parts of Paris can also be found here in the tiny towns of Ré. No real Parisian is going to put up with pizza and burgers all summer long.

The French visitors who frequent Île de Ré (and there are a lot of them), are like the wealthy Americans who regularly flee New York and Boston for Nantucket or Martha's Vineyard, seeking simplicity. They come here to get back to nature: to breathe clean air, cycle, swim, kiteboard and sail…not to sit in a traffic jam in the heat or to queue in beach restaurants in Saint-Tropez that charge a week's salary for a tin bucket filled with raw vegetables dressed up as *crudités*. Île de Ré is not a 'see and be seen' type of place – everybody's too busy doing other things. Apart from the bicycle trails and the beaches and the harbours, there are antique shops and tiny, elegant boutiques, and a plethora of outdoor brasseries, cafés, and seafood restaurants.

In the splendid fishing town of Ars-en-Ré you will find a place that offers much more than what you would normally expect from a hotel in a small town. Le Sénéchal's appearance is deceptive. From the outside the building looks official and old-fashioned, like a post office. It is located in the centre of town, opposite a very distinctive cathedral with a black-and-white painted stone spire. (Since the spire was the highest structure around for miles, the townspeople decided to paint it to resemble a lighthouse so it could act as a beacon for fishermen returning from a stint at sea.)

Inside it's a completely different story. Thanks to the owner and his wife, an architect and a designer, respectively, the interior of Le Senechel is a collection of open-plan loft spaces with high ceilings and minimal partitions that make full use of the island's abundant

sunlight. Finished in shades of off white, dove-grey and ecru, it has that casual elegance that nobody does better than the French.

Despite its stylish, modern interior Le Sénéchal feels more like a laid-back retreat than a hotel. The design of the spaces was all about creating a place that would be as relaxed as possible, especially in the summer, when you can find guests lounging in the shade on the hotel's tiny patios and on the stone steps leading to their rooms, reading books in striped Louis XVI chairs just outside the breakfast room or lying beside the small swimming pool hidden in a walled courtyard. Others jump on their bikes and cycle to the nearest beach, taking advantage of the island's extraordinary network of bicycle paths, discreetly hidden among its wild sand dunes.

Île de Ré is so bewitching that I have often considered buying something here myself, despite the island's strict planning regulations, which limit the changes that owners can make to their properties. I once tried to buy a Napoleonic fort that had been built on a north-easterly facing beach as an early warning station in the event of a British invasion. The owner was a friend of a friend and he was at a loss as to what to do with it. It was a listed Monument Historique so it couldn't be remodelled and as a former garrison it didn't exactly have much domestic appeal. But I thought it was perfect, and I made an offer that was accepted. 'What do you plan to do with it?' the owner asked me when we finally met. 'A vacation home for my family,' I answered. 'Good luck', was his sarcastic reply. Instinct told me to shut up but ego made me give him a detailed description of my plans. 'At the moment,' I explained, 'the roof is not being used at all. I plan to turn it into a huge roof garden in the style of the Riyadh houses in the Medina of Marrakech. The whole thing will be done with tents and plants and curtains and, as these are all considered non-permanent structures, no planning permission is needed.' 'What about the interior?' he asked, 'Not exactly very liveable for a family.' 'I thought about that,' I replied, proudly, 'I plan to build two monumental fireplaces at either end of the space. Because they are for heating purposes, no planning is needed. I'll also install an island kitchen in the middle of the space. Most of it will come from IKEA in kit form, and as it doesn't require any work to the structure…' '…No planning is needed!' he chimed in, enthusiastically.

Invigorated by our exchange, I left the meeting very excited and eager to get on with this fantastic project.

The vendor did, too. The next morning I received a letter, which explained that for family reasons he had decided NOT to sell the property. Apparently, according to the friend who introduced us, he then went ahead and developed the fort exactly as I had outlined.

So I haven't yet managed to buy a house of my own on Île de Ré. In the meantime, however, the stylish, laid-back Le Sénéchal feels like home enough for anyone.

Situated in the heart of a historic Atlantic fishing village on the French
island of Ré, Le Sénéchal blends its history and tradition with style,
comfort and modernity. It's a potent combination, so it doesn't come
as much of a surprise to learn that the proprietors are an architect
and a designer.

Fittingly, in a culture famed for its mastery of hidden pleasures, nothing on Le Sénéchal's front door indicates that the hotel has all the necessary ingredients for a perfect summer sojourn. Hidden behind its conservative stone façade is a small series of courtyards, one of which features a very pretty pool. The rest of these outdoor spaces are used for eating and drinking.

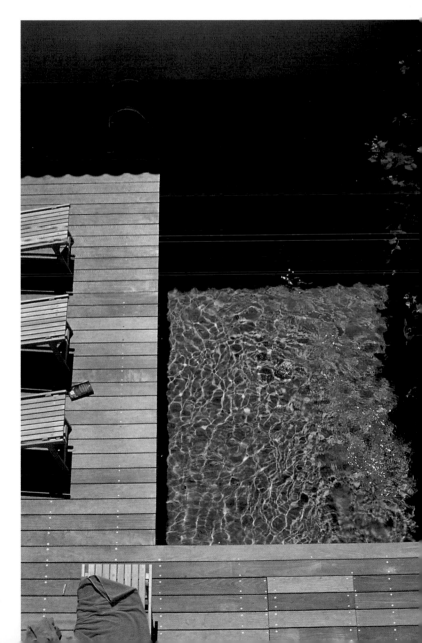

In the centre of town, across the street from Lo Sénéchal, is a church with a distinctive black-and-white painted spire. The story is that the town couldn't afford to build both a big church and a lighthouse, so the residents opted to paint the spire like a lighthouse to serve as a homing beacon for local fishermen returning to port.

PARACHILNA
AUSTRALIA
THE PRAIRIE HOTEL

*Camel sausages and 'roo burgers in a
thoroughly eccentric historic pub marooned
in the Australian Outback*

The Prairie Hotel is situated at the foot of South Australia's Flinders Ranges, the last geological barrier en route to the barren heart of the continent.

This is a vast, empty land of red sand dunes, spectacular gorges, dead forests, sparkling white salt beds, towering purple mountains and endless red plains punctuated by nothing more than the odd shrub. Every cliché of the Australian Outback is present here, which is probably why the area is so popular as a location for films. This is where Harvey Keitel and Kate Winslet were filmed for *Holy Smoke* (1999) and legendary director Philip Noyce came to shoot *Rabbit-Proof Fence* (2002). But apart from making films, why would anyone come to this place in the middle of nowhere? The answer is as bizarre as the place itself. The Prairie Hotel, also known as the Parachilna Pub (after the name of the town) pulls visitors because of its grub. Yes – that's right, a pub, located in what the Aussies themselves would call 'the back of beyond', in a town with a population of seven, is famous for its food. But this is not just any food we're talking about. In a country where food is taken very seriously, the Prairie Hotel has become famous for its cuisine – its 'feral' cuisine, to be exact.

If you would like to sample an antipasto of smoked camel, char-grilled emu, smoked kangaroo and wild goatsmilk curds served with muntry-fruit chutney, followed by a mixed grill of goat chop, kangaroo steak, camel sausages and wallaby shashlik served on a bed of mashed potatoes with homemade gravy, or just grab a 'roo burger or an emu-egg omelette as a quick snack, then you have to make the journey to Parachilna.

And what does it taste like? I think the emu-egg omelette is definitely an acquired taste – not so much from a taste point of view, but more because the egg is just so damn big. 'Roo burger is like a normal burger in terms of appearance and texture but the taste is a bit more like game, and a bit more chewy. Rabbit curry was not my 'thing', but camel sausages, particularly served with the pub's homemade chutneys, were fantastic: meaty and not too fatty, but with a lot of taste. Ross Fargher, the proprietor of the Prairie Hotel (he's the guy on the veranda, with the hat and the beer, on page 179) is passionate about local ingredients, including the myriad wild berries and greens that are unique to his part of the world. It's a journey into regional cuisine and it presents a real reason to make the effort to come here. I didn't love all the dishes but it was fascinating trying them all and I can understand why the Prairie Hotel's 'feral' cuisine has become such a drawcard.

Spectacular scenery and fascinating food are not the only attractions of the Prairie Hotel. Modern architecture is also part of the equation. Behind the traditional stone façade, corrugated roof and lace ironwork of the old pub is a fine piece of eco-sensitive modern design. Devised to provide a cooling system that would not consume vast amounts of energy, the duplex rooms are dug into the ground, each with a bathroom and entrance hallway on the ground floor and a cool, shady bedroom below. It's a clever and appropriate solution for

a place where, in the summer, temperatures often reach more than 50°C (over 120°F). Also, as the structure is part-buried, it doesn't detract from the original stone and wrought-iron Victorian architecture of the pub

As original and inventive as the hotel and its rooms are, few guests spend much time in them when they have the extraordinary surroundings to experience via activities such as a picnic in a dry creek-bed, a cattle drive across the prairie or a scenic flight over the Flinders Ranges.

I took my scenic flight on my way back to Port Lincoln, a remote South Australian fishing town famous (at least in Japan) for its bluefin tuna. My bag was packed and I was wandering around looking for the pilot. 'He's in the front bar,' one of the kitchen staff told me. Only in the Outback will you find your pilot in the front bar.

The pilot, who looked about seventeen years old, was perched on a stool in the old front bar of the Parachilna Pub. Our initial encounter could have doubled as the script for a Foster's commercial.

'Guhdday,' he said with that classic Aussie twang. 'Reckon you're ready to go? Just give us a hand with the plane, will ya?' I understood what he said but I had no idea what he had in mind. Give him a hand with the plane…how? Literally, it turned out. The plane – a small single-engine Cessna – was pointing in the wrong direction for takeoff and he needed me to help him turn it around. It was standing just outside the pub entrance and the locals (all seven of them) turned around on their bar stools to see the 'city boy' (me) help

Wayne get his plane sorted. So I grabbed a wing and pushed, and he grabbed a wing and pushed in the other direction, and when we finished the Cessna was pointing the right way. It all seemed perfectly normal to Wayne but it was my first time manhandling a plane in a paddock and it was clear to me that this was going to be anything but an ordinary flight.

We took off from the field immediately adjacent to the pub and the locals, who by this stage had moved outside to continue watching the live entertainment, raised their 'schooners' in a toast to our successful departure, and then went back inside to continue drinking.

The pilot was an enthusiast, I'll give him that. And his particular enthusiasm was for pointing out 'twisters' – mini-tornadoes swirling up from the desert. With wide-eyed glee, looking like Jack Nicholson in the most scary moments of *The Shining*, he would head straight for them and our tiny Cessna would shoot skywards as if we were strapped to the booster rocket of the Space Shuttle. He was having a great time, whooping and yelling like a crazed participant at a rodeo while I was busy looking for the sick bags. It was like riding one of those mechanical bulls that they have in bars in Texas, except that it was faster, rougher and more dangerous, and with no audience to appreciate how macho I was being.

The rest of the flight proved to be quite tame – scenic and tame. My slightly crazed 'puberty pilot' had run out of twisters to chase and the landscape had changed from a never-ending expanse of red dirt to a multi-coloured collection of particularly pretty mountains (the Flinders Ranges). It turned out that Wayne had an admirable knowledge of these peaks, which are one of the main barriers to rainfall reaching the Outback, and the flight morphed from a ride in a broken elevator to a pleasant bit of sightseeing.

By the time we reached Port Lincoln (also the white pointer shark capital of the world), it was hard to believe that I had almost rediscovered religion less than 45 minutes earlier.

The accommodation wing of the Prairie Hotel combines the signature Australian corrugated-iron construction with the innovative energy-saving solution of burying the entire structure three-quarters of the way into the ground, making it easier to keep the rooms cool in the scorching heat of the Outback.

Rippled red sand dunes with the odd tuft of bush, mini-cyclones called
'twisters' that twirl dust into the sky, abandoned bits of weathered timber
and old iron: these are some of the sights that attract filmmakers to this
desolate patch of Australia, a place that is beautiful despite –
or perhaps because of – its bleakness.

UBUD
BALI

WAKA DI UME

*Rice terraces, temples, art and
applied modernity in the
spiritual centre of Bali*

Waka di Ume is a discreetly stylish and thoroughly contemporary compound set on the verdant steppes of a stunningly situated rice field in Ubud, the spiritual heart of Bali. Surrounded by mountains and jungle, transected by ravines and rivers, it is as exotic as Bali can be. For a visitor it's everything you hope to find: a seductive mix of serenity, spirituality and breathtaking natural beauty.

It's not hard to see why this tiny town in the centre of Indonesia's only Hindu island became the focus of the art scene as well as a spiritual hub.

Waka di Ume offers a springboard into the deep cultural pool that is the community of Ubud, located in the island's central foothills. There are no beaches – only lush jungle and a sacred river. Life revolves around festivals and the temples. The religious culture of this island, adopted from visiting Indian traders centuries ago, is vastly different from that of the rest of Indonesia, which is predominantly Muslim. Not surprisingly, considering its individuality, the island has a natural affinity for arts and crafts and a deeply ingrained tolerance for anything that is different. That's why Ubud has an art scene that was established long before Western artists first started to visit the region in the 1930s.

It's only fitting, then, that both Ubud and Waka di Ume were introduced to me by the daughter of an artist. Anna, a wonderfully witty writer who worked as art editor for my fledgling magazine *Interior Architecture*, was the daughter of Michael Johnson, now one of the most respected and well-known artists in Australia. She had grown up in a loft in New York City long before it became fashionable to do so, long before the neighbourhood morphed into a shopping destination with an all-black dress code. This unusual upbringing gave her a keen eye for art, fashion and architecture, and it was she who suggested Waka di Ume when I mentioned I was planning a trip to Bali.

It makes sense that Anna would like Waka. It's the kind of place an artist would love. It's also very modern, not just in its aesthetics, but also in its attitude. I love, for instance, that the restaurant, whose form is inspired by the traditional longhouses of Indonesia, serves *nasi goreng* (a native fried rice dish with chicken, spices and peanut sauce, and a fried egg on top) for breakfast. It takes courage to make statements like this, even though it makes so much sense. You are in Indonesia, after all, so why not eat a traditional dish – you can have your eggs and toast anytime at home.

This thin sliver of traditionally inspired contemporary architecture is set in the middle of a series of terraced rice fields. You can walk out the door and join a colourful parade of beautifully dressed devout Hindus on their way to a celebration at one of the nearby temples. This is the real Bali.

However, being a 'culture vulture' is definitely not a prerequisite for staying here. Waka di Ume is a great place for doing nothing

in great style and without breaking the bank. But when you're ready to explore them, Bali's powerful spirituality, its wonderful traditions of craftsmanship and the raw energy of its art world are just outside your door.

The Waka brand was created by three young Balinese brothers who were raised, literally, in the world of hotels. Their father built and still owns the Oberoi on the beach in Seminyak. After university the brothers set out to create a collection of Balinese tourist experiences that offered more challenging way to explore the island. They started with four-wheel-drive wilderness expeditions but soon realized that even the most intrepid explorer needs a base.

Waka di Ume was the brothers' first static project, and their first hotel (there are now four further Waka hotels in hidden corners of Bali) and they didn't need to look beyond the family to find the skill sets required for the result. Ketut Siandana, the youngest brother, was the architect of the hotel and it was his vision that created its sophisticated and seamless marriage of tradition and modernity. The other brother, Intut, studied business administration in Jakarta, which obviously came in handy as the brothers started to expand their brand. The third brother, a hotel-school graduate, provides the hospitality expertise and, because he is very interested in food, he takes care of all the F&B. They're a self-sufficient trio but what really sets them apart is the way they go about finding new locations or possible opportunities around Bali. Whenever they get the chance, they get on their Harleys and ride around the island.

I went with them on one of these adventures and it was an eye opener. Not just in terms of seeing a different Bali: the glacial lakes at Gobleg, the highest village in Bali; and the arid north of the island, closest to Java, where the rainfall is held back by the 3,000-metre (9,000 foot) mountains – but also because it provided such a unique glimpse into the spirituality of the people. Every chance they got (at least once an hour) Ketut and his brothers would stop to pray. Not the stern kind of prayer where you drop to your knees and prostrate yourself, but the Hindu kind where you light a candle and provide the god who resides at the shrine with flowers and food and give some alms (money) to the people looking after the shrine. It's a gentle and caring spirituality and it goes a long way towards explaining why the people of this island are so kind.

I will always be indebted to Anna for her faultless instinct. I feel lucky and privileged that Waka was my introduction to Bali. It shaped my connection with this extraordinary island and its beautiful people in the best possible way.

With its flooded rice terraces, many temples and views
of the shrouded peaks of Bali's impressive volcanoes,
Ubud has always been the spiritual centre
of this bewitchingly exotic island.

Waka di Ume is a successful blend of
tradition, luxury and modernity – all in
the right measure. It immerses you in the
real Bali without sacrificing any creature
comforts. The spa, for example, has a
magnificent two-tiered pool surrounded
by terraced rice fields; the restaurant
introduces local culture via its Indonesian
menu and its architecture, which is
inspired by the traditional longhouse.

MARRAKECH
MOROCCO

TIGMI

*Mud walls, Berber rugs and donkeys alongside
unexpectedly contemporary interiors in an
ancient village in the shadow of the
mighty Atlas mountains*

Tigmi is a hippy-esque low-key hangout in an ancient mud-walled village in the foothills of the Atlas mountains. If you're a fan of Paul Bowles's novel *The Sheltering Sky* and want to discover the country he describes so vividly, or if you like the idea of Gnawa music, tajine cuisine and traditional mud architecture in a Berber town where nothing has changed for a millennium, then this is the place for you.

Tigmi, the name of the hotel as well as that of the village, is so isolated and remote that it is difficult to imagine that the city of Marrakech is less than half an hour's drive away. There's no evidence anywhere – no electricity poles, cars or roads – that you are in the 21st century. So ancient is the town's appearance that film director Martin Scorsese chose it as a location for the filming of *The Last Temptation of Christ* (1988). But I knew about Tigmi long before Scorsese got there – all because of the epic adventures of a friend named Gilles Berthomme.

Gilles was a crazy Frenchman who had made some money operating a limousine service in Biarritz. When he finally sold the business he decided to make good on a promise he had made to himself to become one of the first foreigners to live in the Medina of Marrakech, the medieval part of the city, made up of a labyrinth of passageways and alleys, some no wider than a horse, where even the locals get lost on a regular basis. It is urban density on a scale that we rarely see in the West. Add to that the smell of open sewers and the noise that echoes continually through the narrow passageways and you start to understand why Gilles, after living in the Medina for six months, was tempted when friends told him of a place for sale that was even more exotic, 30 minutes out of town, on the road to Tizi-n-Test.

What he bought was a pleasure garden: a monumental folly built by a long-deceased sultan who had owned much of the surrounding area. It was a square hectare of property – surrounded on all four sides by walls 10 metres (30 feet) high – adjacent to the ruins of the sultan's former *kasbah* or palace. Inside the enclosure, the sultan had developed a beautiful garden, like something from Persia, with four 'pleasure pavilions', corresponding to the points of the compass, offering sumptuously elegant retreats from the hot, dusty landscape. In each pleasure pavilion the sultan installed a portion of his harem and when he needed a break he would head to his walled garden, pick a direction (north, south, east or west) and…you can guess the rest.

It's easy to understand the attraction of such a place. But Gilles wasn't a sultan, he didn't have a harem and he didn't have a clue as to how much work would be involved in bringing the pleasure garden, which was as much of a ruin as the palace, back to life.

Over the next few years, I visited quite a few times and the garden certainly looked like it was going to be magnificent. Gilles had planted it with fruit and pepper trees, and had tiled the walkways and water features with spectacular geometric *zillij* (mosaic tiles). The four pavilions were painstakingly rebuilt with walls of shining *tadelakt* lime-plaster finish, ceilings of hand-painted oleander branches, and tiled floors piled with Berber rugs.

Gilles had great plans for his sultanic folly: he dreamed of turning it into a small luxury hotel, and he almost succeeded. When he started the project he had a foxy French girlfriend and a car, but by the time he (almost) finished, he had only a donkey left. It was tragic how close he got, but it was just too much work and eventually he ran out of money. His girlfriend left him, taking her car (their only car) with her. The last time I saw Gilles he was trying to grow crops on the land surrounding his pleasure garden to make ends meet. His face was that leathery texture you get when you are working in the sun all day and he was wearing a *djellaba* that made him indistinguishable from the other poor farmers in the village.

It's difficult to imagine that such a story would inspire anyone to want to attempt the same thing in the same village, but it did.

When I went to visit Gilles, I often brought Max Lawrence, a young energetic Briton whose father was the founder of a pioneering travel company called The Best Of Morocco. Max knew early on that he had had enough of England and schools so he stayed behind in Marrakech and applied his French, English and Arabic language skills to his own property renovation projects. Eventually, in partnership with the son of the famous Moroccan architect Charles Bocarra, he created a hotel called Caravanserai, from a series of mud-walled dwellings on the edge of the Palmerai in Marrakech. The hotel was a success and Max and his partners were looking to repeat it. The

place in which they chose to do so was Tigmi. With the pathological optimism of youth, they bought a sizable chunk of the ancient mud-walled village not far from Gilles's pleasure garden, and began the labour-intensive process of converting it from a forlorn maze of crumbling mud walls into an original and refreshingly contemporary hotel. Working in a place that had never even had electricity, they used mainly traditional building techniques and materials such as rammed earth, *tadclakt* walls, and *zillij* tiling. But they also made sure to incorporate mod cons, installing large, beautiful bathrooms, air conditioning and a swimming pool. Unlike poor old Gilles, they managed to get it finished and, just as importantly, they also hired one of the most experienced and professional hotel managers in Marrakech to run it.

Tigmi the town still looks just as as it would have a thousand years ago, but Tigmi the hotel is a stylishly sophisticated bolthole decorated with traditional Moroccan elements and materials that have been used in a pared-down, bold and contemporary way. I love the way it transports you back to the Morocco that once locked itself away from the rest of the world for over five hundred years, yet you are only a 30-minute drive away from the sophisticated bar and restaurant scene of Marrakech. Morocco is one of the few places left in the world where you can be sipping mint tea in a chic café on Boulevard Mohammed V and 30 minutes later wandering around a dusty mud-walled village.

From a distance you would never know it's there. On the outside, the
whitewashed, crenelated mud-brick walls of Tigmi's ramparts are in keeping
with old Berber traditions from both the Atlas Mountains and the Sahara and
blend in completely with the rest of this ancient village in the foothills. Although
Tigmi's interior still uses Moroccan decorative elements, it is a more modern
affair that places emphasis on space and light.

The guest rooms seamlessly combine signature elements of southern Moroccan culture without a hint of a cliché. The ceilings in the lofty guest suites, for example, have been lined with the traditional oleander branches, which are arranged in the geometric patterns that are a favourite decorative motif in many Islamic cultures. Even the shape of the rooms themselves reflects the traditional Moroccan preference for long, rectangular spaces.

UBATUBA
BRAZIL
POUSADA PICINGUABA

*A tiny fishing village that no one has ever heard
of on a spectacular stretch of jungle-clad Brazilian
coast less than three hours from São Paulo*

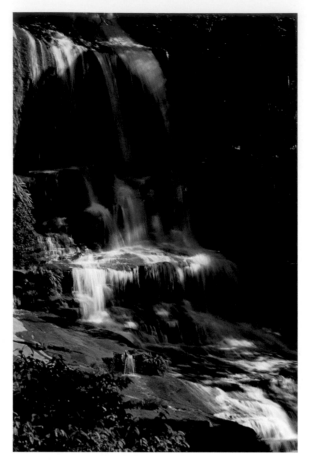

It all started with a comment in the visitors' book.

Andrew Nichols and Ted Wilson, friends of mine from London, had been staying in a remote hideaway in Brazil, an extraordinary place in a tiny fishing village on a remote stretch of the Atlantic Coast about a three-hour drive from São Paulo. When they left they wrote in the visitors' book 'FINALLY – a place that Herbie hasn't been to'.

The proprietor, a young French banker-turned-adventurer named Emmanuel Rengade, was intrigued by the comment. Who was 'Herbie'? Andrew and Ted told him about me and explained the *HIP Hotels* connection and that was it – the proprietor was off like Hemingway after a marlin. He got my number and email address and left countless messages. I confess I didn't answer any of them, as I was busy photographing places in the north of Brazil and my schedule was packed. Nevertheless, he persisted, and even turned up at the airport in São Paulo when I happened to be passing through. He was a smooth talker and – although the last thing I wanted to do after a long flight was to sit in a car for another three hours – I eventually agreed to let him take me to Picinguaba. I was intrigued. Nobody I knew in São Paulo had ever heard of the place. According to the ever-persistent Emmanuel, it had amazing beaches and fantastic surf. Why then, I wondered, would the Brazilians all head to the north when they go to the beach?

It was difficult to make a judgment call, since we arrived after dark, but when I woke the next morning and saw what was outside my window, I was happy I had made the schlep. Picinguaba truly is an amazing place. It is surrounded by verdant jungle, which clings to impressive mountains that cascade in lush greenness down to the vivid blue of the Atlantic. The beaches are pure white; the surf is consistent and – a big plus if you're a keen surfer – there is almost no one else there. To call Picinguaba a town is a stretch: four buildings and about twenty people is more or less the sum of it, in contrast with São Paulo's population of more than 10 million only a few hours away.

The hotel itself has been rescued from what used to be an abandoned convent. (In South America the Catholic Church has always managed to pick the best spots for its houses of God!) It has been converted into a simple and pretty place, decorated with an eclectic collection of native Brazilian artefacts, such as tribal headdresses. It's simple but elegantly so. It looks a bit like a white-walled art gallery, and doesn't do anything to distract from the beauty of the surroundings. But it doesn't lack in luxurious comfort either: all-white contemporary tiled bathrooms, a swimming pool overlooking the sea, and a dining room with sweeping views. It's the kind of balance that the French seem to have a talent for. But Picinguaba is all about the outdoors: surfing, hiking, sliding down waterfalls on your backside, swimming in the mouth of the river where it meets the ocean. Emmanuel and I did it all – in one day!

It was one of the best days – and certainly one of the most action-packed – that I have ever experienced in South America.

Emmanuel brought me back to the airport, as any decent abductor would do, and I boarded my rescheduled flight to Paris, completely exhausted but very happy with my new find: so beautiful, unspoiled and completely undiscovered. I vowed that I would come back. Little did I know that I was bringing a very special piece of Picinguaba back home with me. By the time we landed in Paris there was a strange lump on my wrist and I wasn't feeling at all well.

So off I went, not for the first time in my travelling career, to the infectious diseases clinic at the Institut Pasteur, where the staff were happy to see me again. 'Nothing serious, Monsieur Ypma – take this course of antibiotics [the French cure-all] and you will be fine.' With time, the lump on my wrist turned into a mini volcano, a massive bump with a very offensive crater that would not stop suppurating. It was embarrassing and I desperately needed to cover it for a series of meetings I had planned in London, so I borrowed one of my son's Lucky Luke cartoon plasters. After a long day under the plastic band-aid my wrist felt decidedly worse, and when I got back to the hotel and gratefully ripped the damned thing off, I saw that the entire crater had gone bright yellow – like a pimple – ripe for popping. I squeezed the lump on my wrist, and to my horror a bright yellow worm-like creature covered in little black hairs started to wriggle out of the crater in my skin: I was giving birth to an alien. It ended up writhing in the sink.

The next morning I took my new little friend for a tour of my publisher's office, where reactions ranged from bemusement to repulsion.

It was, it has to be said, a particularly ugly little alien. Then it was back to the Institut Pasteur. Initially the staff were quite excited: something new and exotic from the Brazilian rainforests! But sadly it was all a bit of an anticlimax, as they eventually determined that I had been bitten by a type of South American fly that injects you with its eggs and then uses your body to gestate the hatched larvae. They had, in fact, seen a woman that very morning who had been bitten by the same insect, but *her* little alien had emerged from a massive bump in the middle of her forehead, which was much more dramatic than having it exit via the wrist.

In a way it was fitting that such an exotic destination left me with such an exotic souvenir. What else, other than a bright yellow, squirming, wriggling alien with black hairs, could possible compete with the drama and spectacle of purple jacaranda trees, sweeping deserted beaches, rolling surf and mountains cloaked in deep, green rainforest?

So, despite my mini medical docudrama, I am very keen to get back to Picinguaba. Next time I know to stay longer and to bring some toys. From what I saw of the surf, a 7'6" 'gun' is definitely on the cards, as well as a stand-up paddle board (SUP). Many of the best beaches, the ones I haven't been to yet, are not accessible by road and an SUP is the perfect way to get to coves and bays that otherwise require a boat and planning (although there is a boat for those not interested in paddling for hours).

Perched on a promontory facing a spectacular bay and a local fishing beach, Pousada Picinguaba is all about its mesmerizingly beautiful surroundings. As such, its interiors work like those of a good art gallery. They are comfortable, elegant and welcoming, but allow the views framed by the windows to be the focus.

And what about my abductor, Emmanuel? After six years in Picinguaba he embarked on a second venture, a coffee plantation called Fazenda Catuçaba in the mountains on the way to São Paulo. Now his guests can experience both the charm of a colonial plantation in the mountains, followed by the wild, unspoiled beauty of a forgotten chunk of the Brazilian coast.

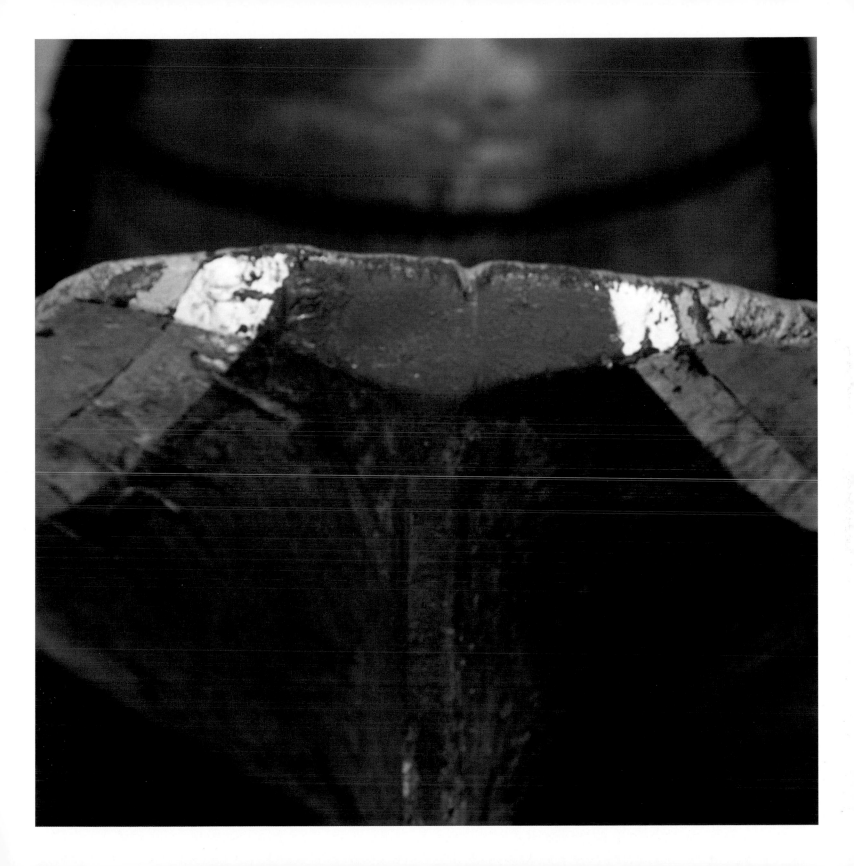

ÎLE DE RÉ

FRANCE

LA BARONNIE

An aristocrat's quayside château
converted into the most splendid B&B
in all of France

There is no shortage of châteaux in France, but they have a justly deserved
reputation for charm and beauty and almost never fail to impress when
travellers are lucky enough to be able to stay the night as paying guests.
But there's only one La Baronnie: a charming former aristocrats' home
in the heart of a picture-perfect fishing village on the Atlantic coast.

Everyone wants the same France. It's the country depicted in charmingly bucolic movies such as *Manon des Sources* or books such as Peter Mayle's *A Year In Provence*. This France has narrow cobbled streets and slightly shabby ochre-washed houses with pale blue or grey wooden shutters that could use a lick of paint. It has a café on the corner where the waiter in the white shirt, black bow tie and smudged apron bangs your Pastis unceremoniously on your glass-topped wicker table and then grins through his Gauloises-stained teeth to let you know that he treats everyone this way. The local market is full of foods you've never seen, including a cabbage that looks like it came from another planet. The cheese section is not taken seriously by locals unless it has at least sixty different varieties. Wooden fishing boats are arranged along a traditional crescent-shaped quay, which is lined with seafood restaurants that have oysters on display only in the months that contain the letter 'R' (when the French consider it safe to eat oysters).

Although the real France often falls short of this idealized country, there is one place that offers all of the above, along with some very beautiful beaches, an extensive network of bicycle paths hidden behind dunes and grasslands and a fantastic microclimate that makes it one of the sunniest places in the country. The reason you have never heard of this place is simple: the French are doing their best to keep it a secret.

Île de Ré, in the Golfe de Morbihan on the Atlantic coast, has been Parisians' summer holiday destination of choice for decades. The island has no tourist development in the conventional sense: no time-share apartment buildings, large hotels or shopping malls. There are only the wild dunes and the beaches, the salt marshes that still produce some of the most sought-after gourmand-grade sea salt, and a handful of fishing villages made up of traditional cottages. That's about it, and both the locals and their Parisian visitors are hell-bent on keeping it that way. Most of the former fishermen's cottages have been converted into summer homes, without disturbing their protected historic status, and that's about the only option if you want to stay on the island. As a result, demand is high and supply is almost always limited, resulting in property prices that rival those of Paris.

The island's most charming village, Saint-Martin-de-Ré, also happens to be its historic capital. Tucked away among the fishermen's cottages and dusty squares where locals play boules, near the crescent-shaped harbour with its wooden fishing boats and quay lined with seafood restaurants, there is a completely unexpected gem of a place for visitors to stay – possibly one of the most exceptional places I have ever found. The address gives nothing away. On a cobbled street lined with fishermen's cottages, in the space where there would normally be yet another cottage, there is a pair of wrought-iron gates, exactly the width of a house, with a bell on the side. Through the gate you can see a small cobbled drive that leads to a copse of trees. There is no hint that when the gates open and you wander down the drive you will find a majestic château hidden in the very heart of the village.

Yet here it is. Built by an aristocrat who was the island's original major landowner, La Baronnie occupies an entire block in the centre of town, discreetly hidden behind a row of cottages on one street and by a very high wall on another. It has a massive garden with plenty of trees and a back door that leads directly to the harbour. I'm sure there is nothing else like it in all

of France. It's superb and splendorous with panelled rooms, hidden turrets, winding staircases and stone fireplaces – but it is also remarkably affordable and unpretentious. The owners of La Baronnie have no desire to turn it into a fancy adults-only Relais & Châteaux-style property.

La Baronnie is owned and run by a very hip couple – Pierre and Florence Pallardy – who make this splendid property their home and for part of the year (April–October) open their countless grand bedrooms to paying guests. They waited for years to get the chance to buy this extraordinary property and spent many more years renovating it. Their single-minded dedication to the project has made this place enchantingly beautiful but their lively personalities have also made it great fun. Pierre, particularly, is quite a character. He used to be President François Mitterand's private 'healer' and he still operates a small clinic on the property. There are many stories about

his special talent for curing people with chronic backache and inflamed joints. Guests who arrive here pale and limping can leave suntanned and walking normally.

There are not many places in the world that give me serious property envy but this place does – not just the building, but the entire lifestyle. I dream of finding another town somewhere on the island that has a similar mansion hidden behind the fishermen's cottages but I know there is only one: a magical place where you can immerse yourself in the very best of France.

I love the idea of holidaying here with children: an entire island safely accessible by bicycle, with pristine, perfect beaches, yet less than three hours from the French capital. In the summer, straight after breakfast, Florence and Pierre head to one of the island's superb beaches, with their sons and all their kitesurfing gear, and guests should do the same. For the parents – in addition to the pleasure of watching their children enjoy the great outdoors – there are also the local seafood restaurants, better than any in Paris, that provide the perfect way to end a day of easygoing bliss.

I'm sure by now you are waiting for the 'but' – something like 'Yes, it's perfect, but there is the fish-canning factory next door...' There is no 'but'. This is genuinely the most perfect B&B in the world: a splendid yet unpretentious château in the heart of a charming fishing town on one of the most picturesque islands off the Atlantic coast of France.

Many places featured in books about authentic French style look like this – but most of them are not places where you can stay the night, especially without paying a fortune for the privilege. No wonder the Parisians have been doing their best to keep La Baronnie a secret.

Character, colour and quirky details define this exquisite abode
as much as its splendid architecture and unique location.
Everywhere you look, La Baronnie is like a picture waiting
to be taken for a postcard.

SICILY
ITALY
ATELIER SUL MARE

*Change your relationship with art forever
at a crazy, fun and original hotel on
the north-west coast of Sicily*

Atelier sul Mare is like no other place on this planet – a wonderfully weird 'out there' experience that is as far away as you can get from a conventional hotel. First of all, there is no lobby – or, more accurately, there used to be a lobby but now it's now occupied by a giant kiln. Yes, a kiln. It's not a case of a utilitarian object being treated as sculpture, but a fully functioning kiln, and guests are expected to use it, preferably as soon as they arrive. Atelier sul Mare supplies its guests with undecorated clay plates, (and cups and saucers and bowls); you paint them in any way that inspires you, shove them into the kiln, and at your next meal your food is served on the 'art china' that you have created.

But wait, the best part is yet to come. After you've finished eating, you can – and it's certainly encouraged by the staff – smash your plates in as theatrical a fashion as you can muster. Throw them like frisbees; toss them over your shoulder; roll them off the table; bash them against each other *Zorba the Greek* style, anything goes, so long as you don't hurt another guest. Then, when your creation is in smithereens, you get to go back to the kiln and do it all again.

There's more…

Atelier sul Mare is a hotel but there are no rooms. Instead, there are three-dimensional art installations…that you can sleep in. Eleven artists were invited by Antonio Presti, the art-obsessed proprietor, to turn what were previously guest rooms into art installations. The only guidelines were that each installation would have a bed, a bathroom, and somewhere for guests to put their clothes…sort of.

There's an all-white 'nest', created by sculptor Paolo Icaro, where you sleep in a cocoon-like egg-shaped concrete structure covered with a bedspread quilted to look like giant feathers. The structure is so large that it takes up the whole room, almost obscuring the windows. But at least it has windows. There's another installation (aka guest room), called 'The Sea Denied', that is entirely panelled in threadbare recycled wooden doors, shutting out any evidence of the hotel being on the water's edge. That is, except for a wall-to-wall bank of television screens that loop a video showing waves breaking on a beach.

There's also a space, conceived by Chilean film director Raúl Ruiz, which consists of a two-storey steel tube, painted black on the inside, with a revolving circular bed at the bottom. You have to crawl to get inside and there's a handle on the wall that cranks open the roof so you can see the night sky. In effect, you are sleeping inside a giant telescope looking at the stars.

My hands-down favourite, however, is the suite created by Presti himself as a homage to Pier Paolo Pasolini, the famous Italian poet and film director. Pasolini lived in Yemen for many years, so the room/installation is entirely covered in red mud accented with a dado of white Arabic writing. He was murdered by being run over with his own car, so the bathroom is a massive spaghetti-like tangle of copper pipes, called 'The Car Wash', which sprays water in every direction when you turn on the taps.

There's more…

Every morning, after breakfast, after the ritual plate breaking, which by now you will be starting to look forward to with relish, guests are invited to throw their room keys into a big marble bowl on the reception desk. Guests can then grab a key, preferably not their own, and take themselves on a tour of someone else's installation. It's fantastic fun and the staff proudly told me that in all the time they have been doing this no one has ever had anything stolen. (All the same, I left my camera bag at reception.)

I could go on and on. There's a bar that used to be a garage until Presti rescued it from mediocrity by asking the local gangs to graffiti it. The result was stunning, and the hooligans were delighted. And that's the point of it all from Presti's perspective. He's convinced that art has been ruined by heavy-handed intellectuals and investment buyers. It dismays him that people are so rarely exposed to art and when they are it is usually in the stifling environment of a museum. He believes that art should be fun and it should make you act like a child. That's why he built a massive three-storey concrete cube on the beach that kids love to climb, and why the heavy front door to the Pasolini suite is designed to crash to the floor and scare the bejesus out of you when you ring the doorbell.

But even the most bizarre installations at Atelier sul Mare cannot compete with the theatricality of Presti's own daily life. 'Loook at me,' he tells his guests, stretching out the vowels for maximum effect and waving his arms like the conductor of an orchestra, 'I live in Sicilia, I build a big sculpture in a big sculpture park and I am the first to do this but the Mafia come to me and say "Eeeehh! Antonio, you build but you do not pay"…' He pauses for maximum drama, and then continues, '…but I say to the Capo, these are not buildings – this is art.' He pauses again and then with a look of total defeat he shrugs and continues. 'The Capo, he goes quiet like a mouse and he whispers to me "Antonio, your art is as big as a house so you pay like a house…*va bene*?"'

So whenever Antonio leaves for an errand, he says goodbye to the chef, the front-desk staff, the waiters, the barman, the chambermaids and any guests he happens to see, because he is convinced this will be his last day. He hugs and kisses them; he cries; they cry and finally, as he steps into his car, he shrugs his shoulders and says, resignedly, 'Eeeeh! What can I do? I live in Sicilia and I didn't pay.' Later in the day, when he inevitably returns, we all celebrate. It's a miracle! He's alive! There are hugs and kisses and tears as he runs around saying hello to everyone and congratulating himself on his good fortune. Even though tomorrow could now be his last day.

He should have his own television show. I'd watch it even though I know how every episode ends.

To get an idea of the scale of commitment to art at
Atelier sul Mare, look no further than the children
playing on the immense sculpture placed at the sea's
edge by Antonio Presti, the hotel's proprietor and
resident mad scientist. I love the fact that he has
invested in art for people's enjoyment and not to make
money. What better confirmation of the true role
of art in society: to stimulate our imagination.

235

LUXOR
EGYPT
MARSAM HOTEL

*The former Italian archaeologists' headquarters,
just a stone's throw away from Egypt's
legendary Valley of the Kings*

Marsam is a small, low-key and wonderfully earthy hotel located at the entrance to the Valley of the Kings, one of the most extraordinary archaeological sites in the world.

While other visitors to the Valley of the Kings have no choice but to take a bus from Luxor and be herded like cattle to the site, guests at Marsam can simply stroll across the street to visit the elaborate burial tombs of ancient Egypt's ruling elite.

Except, that is, for the tomb of Queen Nefertiti, which is open to visitors only on very rare occasions by special invitation from the Egyptian government. I was lucky enough to be part of such a visit the first time I was in Luxor, together with a host of dignitaries and celebrities who had attended a black-tie dinner in the temple of Karnak to celebrate the launch of a new novel by the bestselling French author Christian Jacq. The day after the dinner we sailed down the Nile in a traditional *felucca* – incongruously flanked by Egyptian Armed Forces RIBs painted in camouflage and bristling with combat-ready security personnel armed to the teeth with automatic weapons in order to protect our VIP entourage from any possible terrorist attack – to the Valley of the Kings, where we were to be taken on a very special tour of the tomb of Nefertiti by Zahi Hawass, the (rockstar) minister of Egyptian antiquities. It was a very special honour and as far as I could tell I was the only person in the group with a camera (probably because the security team hadn't noticed my camera case). My mind was working overtime: if I could

figure out some way to break away from the group I could photograph inside the tomb of one of ancient Egypt's most famous queens, a tomb that has never been open to the public and one that has not been photographed very much at all.

There was a large and foreboding sign at the entrance that read 'NO PHOTOGRAPHY'. I assumed it meant no *flash* photography, to protect the fragile 3,000-year-old murals from light. I had my tripod inside my bag, which meant I could do long exposures using only available light. All I needed was enough time to set it up. As we progressed through Nefertiti's tomb I managed to fall further and further back in the group until I was the last one and there was no security behind me. I planned simply to rejoin the group when they came back to exit the tomb.

For the next few minutes – I don't know how long – I was completely absorbed with the task. This was still in the days of film so there was no way to check on a digital screen, and I was working in near-darkness (see pages 239, 242, and 243 for the result). But after a while it occured to me that I could hear nothing: no voices, no footsteps. And then the penny dropped.

What if they were not coming his way? What if, like most of the very complex tombs built for important members of Egypt's ancient dynasties, there were various entrances and exits? I could imagine that the group would re-emerge into the daylight, rejoin the government's impressive security convoy and only realize that one of their group was missing when they arrived back at the hotel – if

they ever realized at all. Convinced that I been left behind, I started to make my way down the last passageway I had seen the group take, followed by a steep staircase and another passageway and another winding set of stairs…

I was lost in the tomb of Nefertiti.

The exclusivity of my status did little to calm my growing sense of foreboding. I didn't know much about ancient Egyptian tombs but I knew that they were equipped with all sorts of traps to thwart tomb raiders…and smart-arse photographers. My plan, if you could call it that, was to keep going forward, or more accurately, downward. The total silence wasn't encouraging, but what choice did I have? The corridors were getting narrower and I was staring to feel a bit claustrophobic (an understatement). I could imagine the next VIP group, years from now, stumbling across a skeleton and a camera bag.

Luckily it was not the first time I had been in a situation like this. My father, who was a geologist, used to evaluate the viability of abandoned mines, and I was occasionally allowed to accompany him on his inspections. Once, in a tin mine in the mountains of Mexico filled with thousands of bats, a key ladder had collapsed on our way down and we had had no alternative but to find another way out. So now I did what we had done then: keep moving forward; don't try to retrace your steps. Eventually I stumbled across a bigger chamber, with an impressively high ceiling, and there, in the far corner, still listening intently to the archaeologist, was the rest of my group. They had not even noticed that I was missing.

My next visit to the Valley of the Kings was nowhere near as adventurous and certainly a lot more relaxed. The Lebanese proprietor of the place I had been staying – an exotically beautiful hotel called La Moudira, situated in the countryside outside Luxor – told me about Marsam. 'Go see it,' she said, 'I think you will enjoy it.' It was with slight trepidation that I re-entered the area that, not too long ago, I had thought I would never leave, but she was right: Marsam is a gem. Until recently, it had been the headquarters and and residence of the Italian government's Egyptology unit, and you can tell: only the Italians can turn a mud-brick box into an elegant abode. The building is simple and authentic but also stylish in a relaxed, effortless way. The walls are washed with a mud render applied in a repetitive textural pattern, and a dash of deep Mediterranean blue on the doors gives it some pizazz. The floors, especially in all the guest rooms, are covered in large white ceramic tiles, and the furniture, though basic, is made from typical materials of the area such as palm fronds and local timber. Fans on the ceiling keep the place cool and an attractive courtyard is shaded by palm, olive and nut trees.

Marsam is the kind of place we all dream of finding: a place of character and style that doesn't stress the budget, in one of the most extraordinary locations in the world. The real draw of this amazing place is that its doors open onto the Valley of the Kings. Even the most glamorous historic five-star hotel in Luxor cannot match that.

It is not physically possible to get any closer to the Valley of the Kings: Marsam literally looks straight
at one of the most famous archaeological sites in the world. The fact that you will not have to take
a bus or even much of a walk to visit the legendary site of Tutankhamun's tomb or Nefertiti's burial
chamber is not something that even the most extravagant hotels in nearby Luxor can match.

Authenticity and simplicity, executed in convincing and appropriate style, define this small and immensely charming hotel, which was formerly the Italian government's centre for archaeological studies in the Valley of the Kings.

RAJASTHAN
INDIA

SAMODE BAGH

*Marble pavilions and Mughal magnificence
redefine camping in a maharaja's
pleasure garden*

Samode Bagh is a chance to camp like a prince, in 250-year- old Mughal-inspired gardens in a remote corner of Rajasthan. It's a stylish and unusual adventure, and a chance to experience a part of Rajasthan's culture and history that is often overlooked.

The Mughal rulers of India, such as the famous Shah Jahan who built the Taj Mahal, were passionate about hunting. During their tiger-hunting expeditions, which could last as long as six months, they slept in tents. But these were no

ordinary tents. Shah Jahan's tent, for example, was more like a mobile palace, large enough to accommodate his ministers, servants, warriors and favourite wives. It was opulent beyond belief: the Shah's personal apartment featured walls of red velvet embroidered with 18-carat-gold thread. The panels dividing the chambers were cut to resemble Mughal arches and there were even spaces set aside for conducting government business. (We know all this because Shah Jahan's tent was recently found, intact, in the basement of Jodhpur's Mehrangarh Fort.)

The other obsession of the Mughal rulers was gardens. In Arabic, 'garden' and 'Paradise' are the same word and the Muslim Mughals adopted the same interpretation. For many centuries Rajasthani royal families built elaborate gardens, with magnificent trees and intricate marble fountains and water features, where they went to escape the heat and held gala events such as weddings and carnivals. The exquisite Samode garden (*bagh*), built more than 250 years

ago by Rawal Sheo Singh Ji of Samode, is a wonderfully well-preserved example. The garden features marble arches, raised pavilions, sculpted trees, immaculate sunken lawns and elaborate interconnecting marble fountains fed by natural springs. It also has a swimming pool, hidden behind a *jali* – the traditional stone-fretwork screen that features prominently in Mughal decoration – finely decorated as a porcelain plate. It must surely rank as one of the most beautiful swimming pools in all of India.

Samode Bagh has cleverly managed to merge two important components of Mughal culture into one extraordinary experience. You get to sleep in an elaborate tent, with panels that imitate the murals of Samode Palace, furniture that evokes the colonial style of the Raj, and the unexpected luxury of an ensuite marble bathroom (this is, after all, a *tent* we are talking about!). And then you get to wake up in a garden that was originally intended to mimic Paradise.

I discovered this exquisite place as per my usual method: dumb luck and smart friends. I was on a road trip for *HIP Hotels*, photographing Samode Haveli, Samode Bagh's sister hotel in Jaipur. While I was there, one of the members of the former royal family of Samode invited me for dinner. He knew about the book I had written about India and he was interested to know what else I had planned. I could feel a bit of railroading coming on, so I started to explain that my schedule was completely committed, which it was, but that I would love to see Samode Palace the next time I was in Rajasthan.

'Oh, yes', he replied in a cut-glass accent that betrayed his time spent in British public schools, 'Yes, it would be nice for you to see the Palace, but it is a real pity that you won't be able to see the Bagh.' Then he began to tell me all about the garden his great-great-great grandfather had built almost four centuries earlier and how it was the kind of completely unadultered, authentic gem I seemed to be drawn to.

Well, I was hooked. I had to see these gardens. The fact that Samode was almost four hours away by car and that I would have to start driving at 2.30 AM to get there for sunrise was irrelevant. The Bagh was calling. It was cold and pitch black when they woke me at 2 AM. The car was waiting for me and at exactly 2.30 AM I climbed into the back seat of my host's tiny off-white Ambassador. Most of the back seat was already taken up by a very tall gentleman with a big beard and a perfectly wound turban. He was to be my guide and he took his job very seriously. From the moment we left Jaipur until we arrived at Samode Bagh he didn't stop talking. I would have preferred to sleep, but I did learn a lot about my destination and the family that used to own most of it.

Samode is a sufficiently remote part of Rajasthan to still offer a glimpse of a way of life that is fast disappearing in the rest of India. Here the men still wear turbans and the women wear bright-coloured saris that seem even more vivid in contrast with the dusty, dry landscape. Ornately decorated camels are a regular sight and in the shimmering midday heat, surrounded by all the gem-like colour, they look like something out of a movie.

But it was anything but shimmering when we first arrived. It was COLD. You forget that Rajasthan has a desert climate, which makes it hot and dry during the day and freezing cold at night. As a result of the temperature difference, there was a faint mist hanging over the gardens, making them look even more spectacular than I had imagined.

The family had not been exaggerating. The gardens were beautiful and the concept of being able to camp in them was as deliciously eccentric as it gets.

In the past three decades, I have been to India at least twenty times. It's a country that never fails to inspire me but I do think one of the most important things to consider is finding a place that can give you respite from the sensory overload that is India. This subcontinent is loud, crowded, dusty, hot, colourful, monumental, tragic and amazing to such a degree that it can be overpowering and exhausting. As a visitor you need a place that shuts the door on the country's cultural cacophony and in all my travels I have seldom come across a more original and effective haven.

A magnificent tent in a Mughal pleasure garden in Rajasthan is more than a pleasant oasis and a memorable travel experience – it's an opportunity to immerse yourself in the extraordinary heritage of Rajasthan, and to camp like a maharaja.

There are tents and then there are Mughal tents. Mughal tents were made for maharajas and had sumptuous chambers and lavish luxuries. The tents in the magnificently elegant gardens of Samode Bagh reflect this tradition. With spacious accommodation, walls made of hand-painted cloth and the unexpected luxury of marble bathrooms, Samode Bagh offers an opportunity to experience camping – maharaja style!

The most pleasant surprise at Samode Bagh is the
swimming pool. It is truly a pool fit for a maharaja and
it must rank as one of the most splendid I have seen.
Even the spaces leading to the pool create a sense
of anticipation and drama – the Mughals certainly
knew how to infuse water with glamour.

AEOLIAN ISLANDS
ITALY
HOTEL SIGNUM

Il Postino *comes to life on the lushest island in the Aeolian archipelago*

Hotel Signum offers an idyllic lemon-scented experience of the Mediterranean. It is a unique blend of white-washed simplicity, authenticity and luxury set around a series of landscaped terraces overlooking the azure blue of the Tyrrhenian Sea, with the islands of Lipari and Stromboli shimmering in the distance. Embedded halfway up the volcanic slopes of Salina, the most beautiful of all the Aeolian Islands, it's the kind of place we all dream about; a paradise straight out of a movie.

That movie is *Il Postino* (1994), a film as wiltingly beautiful as the island on which it is set. *Il Postino* is the story of Mario, the son of a fisherman who doesn't want to follow in his father's footsteps and instead becomes a postman. Practically his only customer as he makes his bicycle rounds on the island is the famous exiled Chilean poet Pablo Neruda, who befriends Mario and teaches him about the power of the written word. Mario is in love with Beatrice, the most beautiful girl on the island, but he has no idea how to connect with her and Pablo, begrudgingly at first, helps him to romance her with poetry. It works so well that they get married and at the wedding the poet gets the good news that he is allowed to return to his native Chile. Mario writes to him constantly but he doesn't get any reply, so he decides to record all the sounds of the island, including the heartbeat of his son still in his mother's womb, and send it to him. Years later, the poet returns to the island and meets Pablito, the child named in his honour, and he learns the fate of his friend Mario, who

died in a Communist rally gone wrong, shortly before his son was born. The film won many critical accolades, including an Academy Award.

Signum, this extraordinary, captivatingly charming little hotel, has more than the island of Salina in common with the film. The entire cast, including Massimo Troisi, the actor who played Mario, stayed here for the duration of the filming.

When I first visited Signum, the owner regaled me all morning long with stories about the shooting of the film, while we sat in the vine-covered courtyard where breakfast is served. As a big fan of the film I was mesmerized by the owner's stories, so much so that my photography, which usually kicks off at dawn, didn't start until late in the morning and then I had to shoot like a maniac to catch up.

I was so completely absorbed in the task that I didn't notice the strained expression on the face of my host when she came to give me a glass of lemonade (freshly made from the lemons growing on the property). 'We did not know where to find you,' she said. 'I'm afraid there was a phone call for you and one of our staff took a message. I'm afraid', she continued, with a devastated look on her face, 'that your sister has died!'

The news hit me like a sledgehammer. My sister was my only sibling and because we travelled so much as children we grew up as best friends. I guess there was always a risk, considering how much I travel, that I would be at the opposite end of the planet when such a thing happened but I never expected to be this far away (she was in Australia) nor that it would happen so soon. She was only forty-three.

The rest of my stay at Signum was a blur. The only thing I could think about was getting back to Australia for the funeral. There weren't many options. At this time of year there was only one ship that did the rounds of the islands before sailing all night to arrive in Naples the next day. This was followed by a flight to London, another flight to Singapore and then a final flight to Adelaide – the entire journey took me three days. In hindsight, I imagine I must have appeared an odd sight to everyone on that ship – a deeply melancholic person in the midst of a boatload of happy travellers on one of the most beautiful stretches of water in the world.

But it did strike me how strangely similar this all was to the film. Mario the postman died before his son was born; the actor who played him died of cancer (aged only forty-one) before he could see his creation onscreen and my sister died before I could share this place with her via my one of my books or even by telling her about it over the phone. Yet, just as for the poet in the film, Salina is one of the places I long to go back to. Perhaps it's a desire for closure or perhaps the island just has a deep natural affinity with the poetry of despair: the flip side of life that enriches your character while it breaks your heart. Even travel with sad memories is still better than no travel.

In my mind, I've been busy planning my return. I want to taste the golden-coloured Malvasia dessert wine that is only made on Salina. I want to get a bicycle and ride along the edges of this verdant isle and hopefully some of the unpaved paths that the postman used to cycle along are still in existence. I want to wander along the pebble beach where Mario and Beatrice started to fall in love and I want to visit the holy sanctuary of the Madonna del Terzito situated between Salina's twin volcanic peaks, and the Church of the Immacolata in the town square of the nearby village of Malfa where Mario and Beatrice were married. In short, I want to do everything Mario the postman does in the movie, including recording the sounds of the island: the shrieking of the seagulls, the crashing of the waves, the yelling of the fishermen. I don't know why. Call it a romantic obsession.

And I want to stay again at Hotel Signum. Since my last, tragic visit, they have added a beautiful pool on one of the terraces overlooking the sea and a celebrated restaurant that specializes in local Aeolian dishes such as handmade mozzarella di bufala with tomatoes, wild herbs and an acid-free olive oil that is unique to the island. There is also a brand-new spa, inspired by the ancient Greek baths on the nearby island of Lipari, that uses the island's geothermal springs as a basis for its treatments.

Still, for me, none of these improvements are the real attraction. Hotel Signum is like a siren because it is sleepy, idyllic, uncomplicated, and beautiful – like the film, like Mario the postman, and like the island of Salina.

Clinging to the side of a steep green
mountain, often shrouded in mist, Hotel
Signum is the perfect Mediterranean retreat.
With its whitewashed terraces, lemon trees
and spectacular view of the Tyrrhenian Sea
stretching out towards the volcanic peak of
Stromboli in the distance, it's no wonder that
this place was chosen as a base by the
cast and crew when they were filming
the hauntingly beautiful *Il Postino*.

265

STELLENBOSCH
SOUTH AFRICA

MARIANNE WINE ESTATE

*The magnificent obsession of a French
winemaker is inescapably infectious*

Marianne Wine Estate is an unusual and enchanting winery located in the picturesque Stellenbosch vineyard region of South Africa. Surrounded by the rocky peaks of the Drakenstein and the Jonkershoek mountains, it must rate as one of the most captivating wine areas in the world. Stellenbosch has won the lottery in terms of its geographical location, with an extraordinary diversity of natural beauty on offer within a relatively small area. Mountains, beaches, whales, penguins, urban sophistication: you can experience it all in a single day. Cape Town, with its great beaches and restaurants, is less than an hour's drive away. The surfing spots on the Garden Route, the famous ocean-view highway that leads to Hermanus – the place where sperm whales come to mate and little black-and-white emperor penguins run around on the beach – are even nearer.

Wine has been made in Stellenbosch since the 1600s, when the Dutch East Indies Trading Company had the idea to offer a new life to Huguenot refugees who had fled France in fear of being persecuted for their reformist religious beliefs. Any Huguenots willing to emigrate to the southern tip of Africa would be supplied with enough land and all the support structure needed – tools, timber, seeds, farm animals, etc. – to make wine, and in return they would be obliged to supply a certain number of crates or barrels of wine to the Dutch merchant naval fleet as a safer alternative to the poor-quality drinking water available to the crew.

The project was successful and as a result the areas near Cape Town, namely Constantia, Stellenbosch and Franschhoek, developed as vineyard regions. You can feel the history in Stellenbosch. Winemaking has been the focus of this area for more than three centuries. No wonder it has attracted the attention of some serious wine enthusiasts – none more enthusiastic than Christian Dauriac, the French owner of Marianne.

He is the first to admit that he does not make wine for a living. His business is blood, not wine. Dr Dauriac owns and operates most of the blood-testing laboratories in France and with the proceeds, instead of buying yachts or jets, he buys wineries. He owns three other wineries in France: Château Destieux and Château Montlisse in Saint-Émilion and Château la Clémence in Pomerol. For years, adding a winery in the Stellenbosch region was top of Dr Dauriac's shopping list. Every few months he would fly down and visit a host of potential properties. He had been doing this for many years before he decided to buy the winery that is now called Marianne.

The name seemed peculiar. I wondered whether Dr Dauriac had named the winery after his daughter or his wife but it turns out to be more patriotic than that. Marie-Anne was the most common name for girls at the time of the French Revolution, and eventually 'Marianne' became the symbol of the Republic. She is always depicted with flowing red robes, in the robust health of youth, wearing the Phrygian cap, the distinctively shaped hat worn by freed Roman slaves.

Dauriac wanted to distinguish his winery from all the typically Afrikaner labels such as Meerlust, Vergelegen or Kanonkop, and Marianne was also seen a fitting tribute to the French Huguenots who came to Stellenbosch in search of freedom.

It isn't just the name that is different. Marianne is not a hotel in a vineyard. Or a hotel that has a small winery down the road. It is a serious winemaking operation where you are welcome to stay, so long as you don't get in the way. I like the fact that hospitality is not the driving force behind Marianne. It makes the property immune to facile Tripadvisor critiques and it gives it real character and attitude. 'We didn't ask you to stay here' could almost be its motto, and I like the cheeky irreverence of it all.

This is not to say that guests are not well looked after. There are two swimming pools, one with a spectacular vista of the surrounding countryside, the other tucked away behind the main cellars. Guests stay in very spacious self-contained apartments that are at least four times the size of the average hotel room. You can even rent the beautiful three-bedroom Cape Dutch-style mansion that is the jewel of the estate.

Even if you are not interested in the winemaking process, at Marianne you cannot avoid it. To get to breakfast, for example, you have to wander through the neatly arranged rows of vines planted in the rich red dirt of the hilly terrain until you reach a small timber structure tucked away in a copse of trees next to a small lake at the other end of the property. This is the vineyard's restaurant, which was purposely built to be as far away as possible from the main part of the winery to encourage (or force) guests to experience the rustic but intoxicating beauty of the well-manicured Marianne vineyards.

Similarly, the guest apartments in the main compound sit almost on top of the grape-sorting and pressing facility – a shiny collection of stainless-steel vats, each the size of a small house – where the surprisingly tiny grapes, or 'berries' as they are called in the trade, are pressed. So, unless someone blindfolds you and sticks plugs in your ears, you cannot avoid getting involved in 'the process'.

'The process' is what Dr Dauriac lives for. For him it's not a hobby, it's religion. Take, for instance, the wooden barrels in which the wine is aged. At Marianne there is an elaborately constructed catacomb of cellars underneath the property that stores hundreds of barrels filled with wine. Dr Dauriac insisted that I photograph them, all the while talking about the barrels as if they were his children. 'They are made for me in France by the best barrel-maker in the business. Of course they are oak. But not just normal oak, French oak, the best for making barrels. How do I know this? Because I choose all the trees myself. How do I do his? By choosing the forest myself.' You have to admire passion and commitment like this – especially when you find out that Dr Dauriac is only able to spend one or two weeks of the year at Marianne, as he has his other wineries to run in France, along with the blood-testing labs. His unbridled enthusiasm for making

fabulous wine is infectious and this is what makes Marianne so special. Normally, wine tasting and forced-march vineyard tours leave me cold. But at Marianne the staff leave you alone, because they're too busy with the very serious 'process' of making outstanding wine. Eventually curiosity gets the better of you and you start to nose around and notice things.

Dr Dauriac may be the passionate preacher but it's his congregation – you, the guest – who benefits. You get the natural beauty of the Stellenbosch region; you get a fantastic climate; you get facilities designed around someone's unrestrained obsession with wine and, like it or not, you will even learn something.

The Cape Dutch architecture of Marianne's guest apartments and pool pavilion
is vivid and distinctive, a timeless blend of whitewashed walls and thatched
roofs set against the vivid blue of the African sky. There are two swimming
pools on the property, but this is the one with the view. You wake up, go for
a swim as the sun rises, then wander through the vineyards to the breakfast
restaurant. It's hard to imagine a more perfect place to stay.

KOH KOOD
THAILAND
CAPTAIN HOOK

*Jungle, mangroves, empty beaches
and floating Thai restaurants on an
overlooked gem of an island*

Koh Kood is Thailand's best-kept secret. Chiang Mai, Chiang Rai, Phuket, Koh Samui, and Hua Hin are well known but who has heard of Koh Kood? Who even knows where it is?

That's the beauty of this undiscovered gem, sitting just below the coast of Cambodia, in a pristine and remote corner of the Gulf of Siam. This island, which is almost as big as Phuket, has hardly any inhabitants and comparatively little tourism, yet its water is clearer, its beaches whiter and its jungle wilder and greener than any in South East Asia. It's exotic, the way Thailand used to be before budget flights from Moscow, Hong Kong, London, Singapore and just about everywhere else turned many resort areas into Asian Costa Bravas.

I discovered Koh Kood in the best way possible: on assignment.

Soneva Kiri, the newest, the most elaborate and the most unusual Soneva-branded retreat (the other two are in the Maldives) had asked me to photograph their property. It is perched on the westernmost tip of Koh Kood and to spare guests the inconvenience of a long drive from Bangkok, which includes at least four hours on a ferry from the mainland, they have set up their own air service. Together with a small team I took Soneva Kiri's private plane (a reliable Cessna Caravan with an interior disguised to look like a very swanky jet), which landed on their private runway, cut into the middle of a tiny island just off the coast of the resort. A Riva-esque shiny mahogany speed boat was waiting to ferry us to Soneva Kiri's impressive arrivals jetty. The combination of luxury and exotic isolation was intoxicating – this looked like it was going to be a fascinating photo shoot.

But the resort wasn't ready. Three thousand Burmese labourers were still working around the clock to get it all finished and though some of the spectacular residential beach villas were completed, a lot of the rest wasn't, including all four of the planned restaurants. As a result, on the first night, I ate in the staff canteen with our crew, including our svelte but grumpy Brazilian model. It was not an experience I was keen to repeat.

I still wanted to get a feel for the island, to get out of the half-finished resort and explore a bit, so the next night I managed to tee up the only local transport available: the back of a pickup truck.

Outside the gates of Soneva Kiri, Koh Kood is still primitive. The only road is a partially paved version of a four-wheel-drive trail; there are no streets and hence no streetlamps and, unusually for Thailand, there are no bars, hotels or shops (at least not ones that we could find as we bumped around in the dark). The pickup truck delivered us to a tiny timber shack on the banks of a muddy river, and, though it definitely had that 'discovery' factor, the food was disappointing and the atmosphere was, as they say in France, *triste*.

Not one to give up easily, I managed to commandeer the same truck the next night and briefed the driver more rigorously. We were NOT looking for a place that tourists would like – we were looking for a place where a local would eat. In other words, good Thai food.

This time, the bumpy ride in the dark ended in the middle of nowhere. There were no lights and no obvious buildings, just a rickety wooden pier sticking out into a muddy, jungle-wrapped mangrove swamp. Floating at the end of the pier was a small wooden boat with a tiny outboard motor and a very young boy at the helm. Off we went into the pitch-black night, down a river that slowly snaked its way through spooky-looking jungle. On the odd occasion that I would mention crocodiles, the boat boy would laugh nervously. He could have said 'There are no crocodiles here', but he didn't. Apart from that it was dead quiet in the boat. Eventually the river started to widen and every now and then we could see the silhouette of a shack on stilts. To get a mental picture, take the river scene from *Apocalypse Now* and morph it with the setting of *Deliverance*.

Then the first palm trees started to appear; the river took one final bend to the left and suddenly we were faced with a sight none of us had expected. On one side of a broad, sandy breakwater where the river met the sea was a huge crescent-shaped, palm-fringed beach. On the other side was a bizarrely festive timber platform, built on pylons above the water, with dozens of tables set for dinner and festooned with countless lanterns.

The boat dropped us at the platform and we sat down at an outdoor table that had a view of the idyllic beach, softly illuminated by the reflection of all the lanterns in the water. To this day, I have not had better Thai food. It was the kind of place where you eat what they are preparing that night, not what's on the menu, and the kind of place you would never tell your friends about. If the chef opened a restaurant in London she would make a fortune. The only person in our small crew who wasn't enjoying the food was our Brazilian model who made a habit of taking her own Tupperware container of boiled chicken and salad along with her wherever she went. No wonder she was so grumpy.

This magical place at the end of the mangrove river was called Captain Hook (what else?) – and, excuse the pun, we were hooked. We went back every night for the rest of our stay. It did not dawn on me until we made an excursion during the day that we could have in fact made our way here from Soneva Kiri by boat instead of rattling around in the back of the pickup truck, and that this splendid restaurant, in the middle of nowhere, was also a hotel. As well as the festive outdoor dining pavilion, Captain Hook also offered unexpected luxuries such as private open-air spa pavilions on the river and thatched guest bungalows facing the sea.

What an extraordinary thing to build a place like this in the middle of nowhere on an island no one has ever heard of, and even more so when you consider how affordable it is. Captain Hook is truly an amazing place that costs almost nothing. If you were a tax fugitive or an infamous despot or just someone sick of the rat race, it's the kind of place where you could hide out for years. For the rest of us even a few days or a week would do. But you had better go quickly, before Koh Kood becomes the next Phuket.

Koh Kood's mangroves are impressive and full of surprises. The impossibly green canopy snakes alongside the water, getting thicker as you move inland and then, just when you think you have reached the edge of civilization, you find that someone has built a funky, completely original restaurant on stilts in the water.

RIVIERA MAYA
MEXICO
DESEO

*Maya pyramids, funky daybeds and an
all-night party scene in a former fishing
village on the Mexican Riviera*

Deseo is my favourite hotel on the Riviera Maya. It's original and quirky and fun, and it manages to achieve what is generally considered impossible in the world of hotels: to be sexy, stylish… and affordable.

The Riviera Maya is a stretch of Caribbean coast on Mexico's Yucatán Peninsula that extends from Cancún to the border with Belize, facing south/south-west towards the Cayman Islands.

Hundreds of years ago this idyllic place, with its powdery white sand, turquoise water and verdant jungle, was part of the Maya empire, hence its modern-day name. The Maya built magnificent temples and pyramids and managed to expand their territory all the way down to Guatemala before their unique civilization crumbled and was reclaimed by jungle. However, there is one remnant of it that you don't need to chop your way through jungle to see. The pyramids of Tulum sit right on the edge of one of the powdery white beaches that have made this stretch of coast the most popular tourist destination in Central America. It's an impressive site and I like the way the Mexican government has not been too fussy with rules and regulations for visitors. A few areas are cordoned off, but by and large you are free to climb all over the pyramid and imagine yourself a character in Mel Gibson's *Apocalypto* (2006).

Today a new kind of empire is springing up on the Riviera Maya. Every major hotel group has built a resort somewhere along this coast, most offering the kind of private-bungalow-private-pool-fusion-cuisine-restaurant-ultra-spa type of experience that investment bankers the world over seem to prefer; the kind of resort designed to keep you within the walls of the compound for the duration of your stay. Sure, you will be pampered and indulged and massaged to your heart's content, but you will see nothing and experience even less.

Rather than these gilded cages, I prefer the ambience and character of Playa del Carmen, a tiny fishing village that was first spotted by Italian visitors eager to get away from the built-up mini-Miami tourism of Cancún. When Italians develop a quaint, beautiful place, they add amenities but they don't wreck the atmosphere. Playa del Carmen doesn't have any high-rise construction: no casinos, no condos, no huge beach hotels that block natural sand movement and cause erosion. Playa del Carmen has stayed small and low-rise and has retained its village feel. While it has the odd shop selling tourist tat, these are significantly outnumbered by Italian restaurants. A lot of little Italian restaurants, in fact – all offering timber verandas, beach views and authentic food.

In the centre of town is a hotel that has completely thrown away the rule book. Created by Carlos Couturier and Moises Micha – the same team that a decade ago created Habita, the first hotel in Mexico City to break the mould of boring business hotels – Deseo has made a big name for itself with its risk-taking architecture and its über-cool laid-back attitude. Since Deseo, Couturier and Micha have gone on to create groundbreaking hotels all over Mexico and

have even exported their style to New York City, with Americano, a funky addition to the Big Apple hotel scene. They work with some of the most innovative architects and designers, but the core ingredient to their success is the fact that they are Mexican. Although it may not be immediately obvious, their own cultural heritage informs what they create. Deseo, for instance, may have white walls and cool details, but the inspiration for the property was the built legacy of the Maya, the unique cultural signature of the Yucatán Peninsula

On the ground floor, for instance, the building is dense, massive, and inpenetrable. It has no windows, no doors and no open space to speak of. It is like the base of a pyramid, a massive monumental stone block that resembles some of the smaller, flat-topped Maya pyramids in nearby Tulum.

Climb the stairs hidden behind the entrance and you arrive in a vast elevated space, reminiscent of the platforms of Maya pyramids where sports were played and sacrificial ceremonies performed. It's an apt comparison, because at Deseo this space is dedicated to a wild communal ritual: it's a twenty-four-hour party zone with a swimming pool, a series of daybeds that are really beds and not just deck chairs that happen to fold flat, a bar, a small restaurant and, from 6 PM onwards, a DJ. Most hotels have a space where guests can party, but Deseo is a party hotel that happens to have some space where guests can sleep. Sleeping is not recommended, however – and with most of the guest rooms arranged around the PPP (Pyramid Party Platform), it's not really practical, either. Not unless you have a sturdy set of earplugs.

But why go to bed early? This is a place with a Latin soul and none of the guests are here on business. Truth is, staying up at Deseo is the easy bit: the music revs up, guest gather for drinks, then sit down for dinner, then go back to the drinks, take the odd plunge in the pool, followed by more drinks. The music gets louder and louder and before you know it it's almost 4 AM.

When the music starts to wind down it's finally time to go to bed. Deseo must be the only hotel that tells guests when to go to sleep instead of when to wake up.

During the day one word describes the place: chilled. Guests reappear at the party platform pretty much in the same order in which they went to bed. Nothing much happens other than eating, some drinking (mainly strong coffee) and a bit of swimming. In the early afternoon most people wander into town to find a perfect little Italian restaurant for lunch, which isn't hard to do. The rhythm of life here reminds me of Byron Bay on Australia's Queensland coast: party late, wake up late, eat late and sleep when you want. Restaurants are open at the strangest hours and there is hardly a soul on the beach early in the morning, unless there's a great swell, in which case the surfers are out en masse.

Deseo is hardly a quiet or remote retreat but it's definitely the most Latin (and appropriate) way to enjoy this extraordinary part of the world.

White, pared-down and unexpectedly modern, Deseo is all about
keeping it simple without losing street cred. That's why the essentials
for enjoying a resort in the sun – including a straw hat, a bunch of
bananas, and sunscreen – are hanging from a clothesline in your
room when you arrive. What did you expect? A gift shop?

ESSAOUIRA
MOROCCO

AUBERGE DE TANGARO

*Nirvana for kite surfers, Paradise for anyone
looking for stylish authenticity on
Morocco's Atlantic coast*

Auberge de Tangaro brings back the sense of mystique and intrigue that has always drawn adventurers to Morocco. Situated on the highest point of a promontory that looks back towards the historic town of Essaouira, the hotel offers a spectacular view of Morocco's rugged and wind-blown Atlantic coast.

Auberge de Tangaro is close enough to Essaouira that it's possible to dart into town for a coffee or an expedition to the *souk*, but far enough outside the centre to offer privacy and seclusion in the midst of stunning natural beauty. A long, dusty road leads down from the compound, with its whitewashed walls and blue-painted shutters, passing grazing camels and abandoned Moorish architecture before finally arriving at the wide, sweeping beaches, whose big waves and consistently strong winds make the area a popular destination for kiteboarders and surfers.

Anyone looking for the more traditional pleasures of Morocco will also find them at Auberge de Tangaro. There is no electricity – even the dining room is entirely illuminated by candlelight and the kitchen runs on bottled gas – but this only adds to the charm and aura of authenticity. Blue-and-white traditional Moroccan *zillij* tiles line the walls of the bathrooms and handmade terracotta tiles cover the floors throughout. Most rooms feature little more than a bed, a table, a couple of chairs and a fireplace. This elegant simplicity seems completely appropriate to the North African climate, evoking a way of life that has lasted for more than a thousand years.

The apparent effortlessness and style of all this betrays the presence of a design-conscious proprietor. (It's not surprising to learn that he is Italian.) He converted what was once a brothel on the outskirts of town – further testament to Auberge de Tangaro's discreet location – into a hideaway that sums up exactly why real travellers are drawn to this part of the world. Mod cons such as Wi-Fi and satellite television would ruin the place. The pure simplicity of it all forces you to savour and enjoy the subtleties and nuances of the surroundings: the dry salty air, the abundance of fish on offer at the town's markets, the Portuguese colonial architecture and the unique fusion of Berber and Islamic culture.

Essaouira itself has quite a varied history. It was once a closely guarded secret of the Roman Empire. On an island just off the coast, mollusks were crushed to make a rare purple dye, which was used exclusively to colour the robes of the emperor and the capes of centurions. The source of the dye and the process of making it were considered state secrets worthy of protection. In the 16th century, Essaouira was reinvented as a trading port by the Portuguese. The town retains so much of its colonial architecture from this period that Orson Welles chose it as a location for his his film version of Shakespeare's *Othello* (1952). But the history the locals seem most proud of is that Jim Morrison, legendary party animal and lead singer for the group The Doors, once spent an entire summer here in the 1960s. Nobody seems to remember where he stayed (and most

probably neither did he!) but the story is an important part of Essaouira's culture. It gives the town its bohemian street cred and contributes to its reputation for being Africa's answer to Bali. The rock stars have been replaced by surfers but the Hippy Luxe ambience still prevails. People are laid-back and friendly; there's a lively café scene and the cost of living is a lot lower than in Marrakech.

To be honest, my first trip to Essaouira was not a huge success. It was also my first visit to Morocco, the result of a last-minute decision to join a bunch of people who had rented an exceptional house in the Palmerai of Marrakech. Our flight arrived in Marrakech just after dark. We were looking forward to getting to the house and everyone zoomed through Customs and Immigration to meet the car and driver waiting outside. Everyone, that is, except me.

I had been arrested for not having a visa. A week earlier you hadn't needed one but because of some diplomatic row with the Dutch government over the pension status of Moroccan immigrants in the Netherlands, Morocco had retaliated by insisting that Dutch citizens would need a special travel visa for Morocco. The fact that none of the travel agencies or even the Dutch embassies knew this was not deemed relevant. My laid-back attitude had caught up with me: I only had a Dutch passport because I had been too lazy to get an American or an Australian one. After a few tense hours and a fair bit of yelling at me, the Moroccan officials decided to admit me – in exchange for a paying a cash fine.

Marrakech, however, was worth the trouble. It's an intoxicatingly exotic place, and after a few days of acclimatizing to southern Morocco, the braver members of our group decide to organize an excursion to Essaouira. The drive from Marrakech took about three hours and we arrived just before lunch. We wandered around the old town, visited the *souk* and then decided to find a good place for seafood. We were beside the ocean, so we reasoned that the fish must be fresh, but by the time we got halfway back to Marrakech 'Delhi Belly' had struck with a vengeance. Driving in Morocco is one thing; driving with the 'double disasters' caused by seafood poisoning is not something you would wish on your worst enemy. What we would have given that day for a service station with clean toilets!

The second time I visited Morocco's Atlantic coast, the memory was still seared in my mind. Friends wanted to visit the harbour of Essaouira and see the fishing fleet and I obliged, but the smell reminded me a lot of my first visit. It was also a sharp reminder of one of Auberge de Tangaro's little-known but nonetheless important benefits. The old town of Essaouria is charming and authentic, but when the wind blows in a certain direction, which it often does, the town is bathed in the fragrance that comes with being one of North Africa's busiest fishing ports. Auberge de Tangaro, thankfully, is upwind of the port and far enough out of town to not be affected.

Wind, sand and sun at hippy-era prices: Auberge de Tangaro is a fresh take on the exotic escape.

There's a mystical magic about southern Morocco that makes it more than the sum of its parts. Authors continue to be compelled to write about it; musicians have been inspired by it and travellers are attracted to it. Simple objects and ordinary architectural shapes somehow become strangely exotic. Auberge de Tangaro is special: the kind of amazing place that can never be fully explained.

Etnia Pousada
Rua Principal no. 25
Caixa Postal 142
Trancoso
Bahia 45818-000
Brazil
+55 (73) 3668-1137
etniabrasil@etniabrasil.com.br
http://www.etniabrasil.com.br/

The Apsara
Ban Phanluang
Luang Prabang 06000
Laos
+856 71 254 670
info@theapsara.com
http://www.theapsara.com/

Château de Massillan
Chemin Hauteville
Uchaux 84100
France
+33 (0)4 90 64 51
reservation@chateau-de-massillan.com
http://www.chateau-de-massillan.com/

Albergo da Giovanni
Via di Mezzo Franco 10
Località Giglio Campese 58012
Isola del Giglio
Italy
+39 (0)564 804010
http://www.albergodagiovanni.it/

Shali Lodge
Midan El Souk
El Seboukha Street
Siwa, Matruh
Egypt
+20 46 4602399

La Maison du Bassin
5 rue des Pionniers
33950 Lège-Cap Ferret
France
+33 (0) 556 606 063
lamaisondubassin@gmail.com
http://www.lamaisondubassin.com/

Muang Kulaypan
100 Moo 2
Chaweng Beach
Bophut
Koh Samui
Suratthani 84320
Thailand
+ 66 (0)77 422 305
reservation@kulaypan.com
http://www.kulaypan.com/

Satri House
057 Photisarath Road
Ban Thatluang
Luang Prabang 06000
Laos
+856 71 253 491
info@satrihouse.com
http://www.satrihouse.com/

Fort Tiracol Heritage Hotel
Tiracol 403524
Pernem
Goa
India
+91 (0) 2366 227631/ (0) 9767429919
forttiracol@yahoo.com
http://www.forttiracol.com/

La Posada del Faro
Calle de la Bahia Esq. Timonel
Faro José Ignacio
Uruguay
+598 4486 2110
http://www.posadadelfaro.com/

Le Manoir
Île de Port-Cros
83400 Hyères
France
+33 04 94 05 90 52
http://www.hotel-lemanoirportcros.com/

Korakia Pensione
257 S. Patencio Road
Palm Springs, California 92262
USA
+1 760 864 6411
http://www.korakia.com/

Waka Nusa
Nusa Lembongan
(Lembongan Island)
Bali 80771
Indonesia
http://wakanusa.com/

Rancho De La Osa
P.O. Box 1
Sasabe, Arizona 85633
USA
+1 520 823 4257
osagal@aol.com
http://www.ranchodelaosa.com/

Hotel Raya
Via S. Pietro
98050 Panarea
Sicily
Italy
+39 090 983013
info@hotelraya.it
http://hotelraya.it/

Lagoona Davina
TC68/2054 Pachalloor Village
Trivandrum 695 027
Kerala
South India
India
+91 471 238 0049 / 238 3608
finddavina@hotmail.com
lagoonadavina@hotmail.com
http://www.lagoonadavina.com

Le Sénéchal
6 rue Gambetta
17590 Ars-en-Ré
France
+33 (0)5 46 29 40 42
hotel.le.senechal@wanadoo.fr
http://www.hotel-le-senechal.com/

The Prairie Hotel
Corner of High Street and West
Terrace
Parachilna, South Australia 5730
Australia
+1 800 331 473
reservations@prairiehotel.com.au
http://www.prairiehotel.com.au/

Waka di Ume
Jl. Suweta
Br. Sambahan
Ubud 80571
Bali
Indonesia
http://wakadiume.com/

Tigmi
Douar Tagadert el Kadi
Km 24 Route d'Amizmiz
Région de Marrakech
Morocco
+212 (0) 524 48 40 20
info@tigmi.com
http://www.tigmi.com/

Pousada Picinguaba
Rua G, 130
Vila Picinguaba
Ubatuba
SP 11680-000
Brazil
+ 55 12 3836 9105
info@picinguaba.com
http://www.picinguaba.com/

La Baronnie
17 & 21 rue Baron de Chantal
17410 Saint-Martin-de-Ré
France
+33 (0) 5 46 09 21 29
info@hotel-labaronnie.com
http://www.hotel-labaronnie.com/

Atelier sul Mare
Via Cesare Battisti, 4
98070 Castel di Tusa
Messina
Italy
+39 (0)921 334 295
info@ateliersulmare.it
http://www.ateliersulmare.it/

Marsam Hotel
Qurna
West Bank
Luxor
Egypt
+20 952 372 403
marsam@africamail.com

Samode Bagh
Fatehpura Bansa
Samode 303806
Jaipur
Rajasthan
India
+91 1423 240235
http://www.samode.com/bagh/intro.html

Hotel Signum
Via Scalo, 15
98050 Malfa
Salina
Messina
Italy
+39 (0)90 9844222/4375
info@hotelsignum.it
http://www.hotelsignum.it/

Marianne Stellenbosch
Marianne Wine Estate
Valley Road, off R44
Stellenbosch 7599
Republic of South Africa
+27 21 875 5040
info@mariannewinefarm.co.za
http://www.mariannewinefarm.co.za/

Captain Hook
23/1 Rat-Uthid Road
Bangpha
Meung
Trat 23000
Thailand
+66(0)2966-1800-2
info@captainhookresort.com
http://www.captainhookresort.com/

Deseo
5a Avenue y Calle 12
Playa del Carmen
Quintana Roo
Mexico 77710
+52 55 5282 2199
contact@hoteldeseo.com
http://www.hoteldeseo.com/

Auberge de Tangaro
Domaine de Mogador
Quartier Diabat
Essaouira
Morocco 44000
+212 (0) 524 784 784
aubergetangaro@gmail.com
http://www.aubergetangaro.com/

First published in 2013 in hardcover in the United States of America by
Thames & Hudson Inc., 500 Fifth Avenue, New York, New York 10110

thamesandhudsonusa.com

Library of Congress Catalog Card Number 2012944889

ISBN 978-0-500-51674-4

Printed and bound in China by C&C Offset Printing Co., Ltd